Teen Sexuality

Look for these and other books in the Lucent
Overview Series:

Abortion
Acid Rain
Adoption
Advertising
Alcoholism
Animal Rights
Artificial Organs
The Beginning of Writing
The Brain
Cancer
Censorship
Child Abuse
Cities
The Collapse of the Soviet Union
Dealing with Death
Death Penalty
Democracy
Drug Abuse
Drugs and Sports
Drug Trafficking
Eating Disorders
Elections
Endangered Species
The End of Apartheid in South Africa
Energy Alternatives
Espionage
Euthanasia
Extraterrestrial Life
Family Violence
Gangs
Garbage
Gay Rights
Genetic Engineering
The Greenhouse Effect
Gun Control
Hate Groups
Hazardous Waste
The Holocaust

Homeless Children
Illegal Immigration
Illiteracy
Immigration
Memory
Mental Illness
Money
Ocean Pollution
Oil Spills
The Olympic Games
Organ Transplants
Ozone
The Palestinian-Israeli Accord
Pesticides
Police Brutality
Population
Prisons
Rainforests
Recycling
The Reunification of Germany
Schools
Smoking
Space Exploration
Special Effects in the Movies
Sports in America
Suicide
Teen Alcoholism
Teen Pregnancy
Teen Sexuality
Teen Suicide
The UFO Challenge
The United Nations
The U.S. Congress
The U.S. Presidency
Vanishing Wetlands
Vietnam
World Hunger
Zoos

Teen Sexuality

by Don Nardo

LUCENT
BOOKS

LUCENT *Overview Series*

LUCENT *Overview Series*

Library of Congress Cataloging-in-Publication Data

Nardo, Don, 1947–
    Teen sexuality / by Don Nardo.
        p.   cm. — (Lucent overview series)
    Includes bibliographical references and index.
    Summary: Examines various aspects of teenage sexuality,
including teen pregnancy and parenthood, school health clinics,
homosexuality, and sex education.
    ISBN 1-56006-189-8 (alk. paper)
    1. Sex instruction for teenagers—United States—Juvenile
literature.   2. Teenagers—United States—Sexual behavior—
Juvenile literature.   [1. Sex instruction for youth.]   I. Title.
II. Series.
HQ35.N33   1997
306'.7'0835—dc20   96–8696
                                                        CIP
                                                         AC

Copyright © 1997 by Lucent Books, Inc.
P.O. Box 289011, San Diego, CA 92198-9011
Printed in the U.S.A.

Contents

Introduction

TEENAGERS' ENGAGING IN sexual behavior is not a new phenomenon. In every preceding generation at least some teenagers were sexually active. Typically, the parents and teachers of these young people, as well as local medical authorities and community leaders, were concerned about the possible consequences of such behavior, especially unwanted teen pregnancy, abortion, and exposure to venereal diseases, now generally referred to as sexually transmitted diseases (STDs). Such concerns are more prevalent today than ever. All across the United States, large numbers of parents, health officials, and others concerned about sexual issues affecting teens fear the rate of teen sex is increasing and worry about the consequences for young people, their families, and their communities.

In addition to the rising levels of concern from parents and society, the past several decades have witnessed an even more marked change in attitudes toward teen sex, part of a larger transformation of the public climate surrounding the overall subject of human sexuality. Up until the advent of what was called the social and sexual revolution of the 1960s, open talk about sexual topics was generally considered impolite or socially unacceptable. The media, including books, magazines, radio, TV, and movies, consistently promoted a wholesome view of American life. For example, in popular television shows of the 1950s, such as *Father Knows Best* and *The Donna Reed Show*, married couples typically slept in separate single beds, so they wouldn't appear too sexually suggestive. The sexuality of the teenage children of these couples was never addressed either. These young people were never realistically shown as sexual beings who tried both to cope with and to channel their naturally strong sexual urges in a healthy way or who had to deal with the consequences of acting on those urges.

In that same era, the subject of teenage sexuality was generally as taboo in real families and communities as it was in the media. Parents who discovered their children had engaged in premarital sex usually expressed shock, outrage, and dismay; they tried to conceal any consequences of their behavior. Young pregnant girls, for instance, were often forced against their will to quit school, have abortions, or give up their babies for adoption in order to spare their families notoriety, or public attention, and scandal.

Sexual openness—too much or not enough?

Today, by contrast, all branches of the media regularly discuss, gossip about, or dramatize a wide variety of sexual topics, including teen sexuality. Such television shows as *My So-Called Life* and *Party of Five* realistically depict teenagers attempting to cope with explicit sexual issues, such as sexual experimentation versus chastity, contraception, abortion, and homosexuality. And in everyday life a majority of people, including teenagers, tend to talk and joke about sexual topics much more openly and frankly than ever before. Far from hiding their condition, many pregnant teens stay in school right up to their delivery time; some schools even have day-care centers to look after the babies, so young mothers can finish their educations.

Opinions vary on whether such open attitudes about sex are healthy and constructive or unhealthy and corrupting. One side of the debate has people who believe too much openness has led to a casual acceptance of most kinds of sexual behavior and their consequences. According to this view, the modern sexual revolution has promoted and increased irresponsible sexual behavior and attitudes among whole generations of teens, threatening to undermine

After finishing their classes, teenage mothers pick up their children from an in-school day-care center. Such centers are becoming increasingly common in the United States.

traditional religion and the very fabric of the American family and community. "The Sexual Revolution has passed from what people think to what they do," wrote Jesuit priest and Fordham University professor Francis Canavan in 1993:

> Among large numbers of Americans, young ones in particular, the sexual drive has slipped its moorings in Christian morality, and is now regulated, if at all, by vague principles such as respect for the feelings of other people. No sexual conduct is regarded as wrong in itself, but only insofar as it exploits others. . . . The Sexual Revolution is a social revolution whose effects cannot be isolated from the well-being of society at large. The breaking of the link between sexual activity and procreation [reproduction] has already changed relations between men and women, weakened the bond between husbands and wives, and contributed to the disintegration of the family.

The other side of this debate has those who believe openness about sex is healthy, partly because people become exposed to factual knowledge, which they need to make responsible choices and decisions regarding sexual issues. This viewpoint holds that ignorance about various aspects of sexuality—especially among teens—is the main cause of unwanted pregnancies, abortions, the spread of STDs, and other sex-related social problems. "Nobody should make assumptions about what kids know about sex," says journalist Judith Levine. "Research shows that while they're highly aware of sex generally, they're often pretty ignorant about the details. Good sex education is safe sex education too."

The bulk of recent statistics from around the world support the idea that open, frank attitudes about sex, among both teens and adults, promote responsible sexual behavior. A recent editorial in *Glamour*, a popular magazine among

These fourteen-year-olds kissing good-bye illustrate how open many teenagers have become about publicly expressing their sexuality.

The casual acceptance by so many young people of sexually explicit rock music lyrics and videos is another sign of today's openness about sexuality.

teenage girls, calls for continued and increased openness, stating:

> To end up with fewer unwanted pregnancies, we must be more open about sex. Study after scientific study bears this out. A 1994 World Health Organization (WHO) report found that countries with the most open social attitudes about sex have the lowest birthrates, and countries that teach schoolkids about birth control have the lowest teen pregnancy rates. Almost all such studies find that frankness about sex doesn't encourage people to have sex earlier or more often, but it does encourage them to have sex more responsibly.

Tough dilemmas and decisions

Whatever people may think about today's openness regarding sexual issues and themes, frank attitudes and depictions are certainly here to stay. This means parents and others concerned about teen sexual activity and its consequences can no longer deal with these realities by hoping, or pretending, they do not exist or by trying to conceal them. Instead, they must accept that teenagers, like adults, are sexual beings who often face tough dilemmas and decisions about sex. Such decisions include falling in love, becoming sexually active because of peer pressure, the possibility of catching and/or spreading STDs, the confusions and fears that often accompany having homosexual feelings, and dealing with an unwanted pregnancy. This book explores some of the most important and common teenage sexual issues and problems and examines how teens, their parents and teachers, and society in general attempt to cope with such problems and to promote responsible behavior in today's sexually open society.

1

The Scope and Causes of Teen Sexual Activity

PARENTS, TEACHERS, HEALTH professionals, and others concerned about the issues surrounding sexually active teenagers usually begin by asking two seemingly simple questions: First, how many teens are having sex? Second, why did these young people become sexually active in the first place? Answering the first question, they hope, will reveal the scope of the problem; answering the second question may provide insights about how to deal with the problem.

Researchers who study sexual behavior invariably report that these and other questions about teenage sexuality are far from simple to answer. Collecting accurate and meaningful statistics about sex, including teen sex, is difficult. Most surveys and studies include a few thousand teenagers at best, groups, some critics argue, which may not reliably reflect the behaviors and attitudes of society at large.

Even when the researchers are certain their participants represent a fair cross section of society, other factors may distort or confuse the data. When asked at what age they first had sex, for instance, some people exaggerate or lie. And assuming all participants in a given survey respond truthfully, their varied backgrounds must be considered. For example, members of different genders, races, and

ethnic groups often report significantly different average ages for their first sexual experiences.

In addition, researchers have found no simple and easy answer to the question of why teenagers first become sexually active. Those interviewed typically cite a wide variety of social, personal, and emotional reasons, ranging from being in love to curiosity to peer pressure. Most experts believe no two cases are alike and a varied, complicated mix of factors—many of them social and cultural—influences each young person's decision to begin having sex. This makes trying to separate and deal with any single factor a difficult, if not impossible, task. Despite these difficulties, those concerned about the problems continue to study both groups and individuals in a sincere attempt to recognize and understand the scope and the causes of teenage sexual behavior.

This sixteen-year-old boy and his fifteen-year-old girlfriend say they are "in love," which is one of the most common motives teens give for having an intimate sexual relationship.

Sex at increasingly younger ages

The incidence of sexual activity among American teens and the immediate consequences of this activity appear large-scale. Averaging the results of various studies and surveys revealed that in 1993 as many as 10 million

This couple exemplifies the increasingly younger ages of today's teenage lovers. She is fourteen; he is thirteen.

teenagers engaged in at least 125 million acts of sexual intercourse. These acts produced over 1 million pregnancies, resulting in over 400,000 abortions, 130,000 miscarriages, and nearly half a million live births. Of the births, almost two-thirds were out of wedlock. In addition, more than 3 million teenagers contracted STDs such as gonorrhea and chlamydia, and at least several hundred contracted human immunodeficiency virus (HIV), the virus that causes AIDS.

These figures are general, of course, and, by themselves, are not really helpful. Teenagers, after all, do not compose a monolithic group where all members exhibit the same background, interests, desires, and experience. To say ten million teenagers have sexual intercourse in a given year does not explain at what average age they first have sex, if that age is significantly younger or older than that of their counterparts in previous generations, if today's teens tend to experiment with sex only once or twice before marriage or if they engage in it more regularly, if boys have sex more often than girls or vice versa, or if teens from different races and ethnic groups engage in sex more or less often than others.

Regarding the age of first sexual intercourse, all studies show a steady decline in that age, for both males and females, over the past four decades. In the 1940s and 1950s, for example, fewer than 30 percent of young women age eighteen had ever had sex. By 1984, more than 50 percent of those eighteen-year-old females surveyed reported having had sex, and by the early 1990s, according to some studies, that proportion was close to 70 percent. At the same time, the proportion of fifteen-year-old girls who had engaged in sex at least once rose from just 5 percent in 1970 to 27 percent in 1988 and to 32 percent in the early 1990s. Young men consistently reported having sex at slightly younger ages than young women. In the early 1990s, for example, 49 percent of boys age fifteen claimed to have experienced sexual intercourse at least once, compared with the 32 percent of girls who made the same claim.

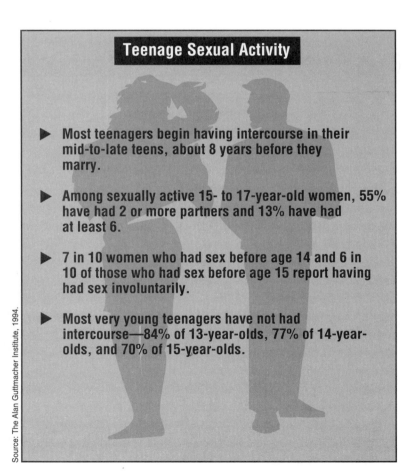

Teenage Sexual Activity

▶ Most teenagers begin having intercourse in their mid-to-late teens, about 8 years before they marry.

▶ Among sexually active 15- to 17-year-old women, 55% have had 2 or more partners and 13% have had at least 6.

▶ 7 in 10 women who had sex before age 14 and 6 in 10 of those who had sex before age 15 report having had sex involuntarily.

▶ Most very young teenagers have not had intercourse—84% of 13-year-olds, 77% of 14-year-olds, and 70% of 15-year-olds.

Source: The Alan Guttmacher Institute, 1994.

Defining "sexually active"

The phrase "at least once" appears to have an important bearing on the data used to define the label "sexually active." Many adults use this label to describe teens who admit to having tried sex, assuming the first sexual experience leads immediately to regular and frequent sexual activity. This assumption is not supported by the evidence, though. Commenting on a study released in 1992 by the Centers for Disease Control and Prevention (CDC), behavioral scientists Susan Newcomer and Wendy Baldwin write:

> Once adolescents report ever having had intercourse, they become "sexually active," even though at least 10% of nonvirgins wait at least a year between first intercourse and the next time they have sex; fewer than one-half have sex again within a month. In the 1992 report, though 54% of students in grades 9–12 reported ever having had sexual intercourse, only 39% said they had had sex within the past three months. Clearly, fewer youth are "sexually active" than have ever had sex.

Regarding initial sexual experiences and the frequency of sexual activity thereafter, significant differences clearly exist among teens of different ages and genders. Some studies have also revealed marked differences in sexual activity for teens from various racial and ethnic groups. More young blacks, for instance, claim to have had sex more often and at younger ages than young whites. A 1988 study by the National Survey of Family Growth found that 54 percent of black girls age sixteen had engaged in sex at least once, as compared to 39 percent of white girls the same age. The 1994 results of the "Sex in America" study conducted through the National Research Opinion Center at the University of Chicago also pointed to noticeable differences between rates of sexual activity in white teens and minority teens. According to the authors of the study, of the teenagers interviewed,

> Half of all black men had intercourse by the time they were fifteen [compared with only a quarter of white men of that age], half of all Hispanic men had intercourse by the time they were about sixteen and a half, half of all black women had intercourse by the time they were nearly seventeen, and

half the white women and half the Hispanic women had intercourse by the time they were nearly eighteen.

Nearly all the studies agree that such differences diminish and eventually disappear by the end of the teenage years. Today, by age nineteen, about four out of five people, regardless of gender, race, or ethnicity, have experienced sex at least once, in most cases out of wedlock. And by age twenty-two, at least 90 percent of those in all groups, the majority still unmarried, have had sex. Whether or not these data reveal an alarming trend or just the natural state of affairs remains a matter of personal interpretation and opinion. The "Sex in America" study offers this general and unbiased comment: "Since the average age of marriage [in the United States] is now in the mid-twenties, few Americans wait until they marry to have sex."

A casual attitude toward sex

Mere statistics that report who is having sex and how often are only part of the picture. Individuals and groups who see an increasing number of teenagers' experimenting with sex as an alarming trend are most interested in *why* teens decide to experiment, especially at young ages. In an attempt to provide this information, in recent years most major studies and surveys have included questions asking about the reasons sexually active teens began having sex in the first place.

The most common reason given by teenagers for becoming sexually active is a combination of curiosity about sex and a personal feeling of being "ready" to have sex; fully half of the teens interviewed for the "Sex in America" study, for example, cited these reasons. This feeling of readiness for sex is partially motivated by a majority of young people, including teenagers, who view sex before marriage as socially acceptable today and, therefore, as an area open to experimentation. This rather casual attitude toward sex contrasts sharply with the viewpoint of teens in the 1930s, 1940s, and 1950s, a majority of whom believed premarital sex was socially unacceptable.

The reasons for this shift in attitude in the second half of the century are somewhat unclear but, in some degree, they relate to the general trend toward more openness about sex and sex-related topics during and after the social revolutions of the 1960s.

Researchers and concerned observers have suggested a variety of more specific factors contributing to teenagers' increasingly casual attitudes toward sex. Some observers emphasize what they see as more open and explicit depictions of sex in the media. According to this view, since the 1960s, popular songs, radio and television shows, magazines, and movies have all markedly relaxed their standards about discussing sexual topics and showing sexual acts. Critics often single out sexually explicit lyrics in songs by many rock and rap groups, graphic sexual images in rock videos by pop icons like Madonna, suggestive poses by young models in print ads and TV commercials for jeans and underwear, and overt or suggestive depictions of sexual acts in TV soap operas and major motion pictures. "The media has become more explicit about sexual behaviors," say social researchers Debra Haffner and Marcy Kelly:

> In an analysis of specific sexual content in prime-time television, the investigators identified approximately 20,000 scenes of suggested sexual intercourse and behavior, sexual comments, and innuendoes in one year of evening television. Sex on the afternoon soap operas is even more prevalent—and almost all sexual encounters on the soaps are between people who are not married to each other. During the late 1970s, there was a four-fold increase in flirtations and seductive behaviors on TV, a five-fold increase in the number of sexual innuendoes, and almost a doubling of the number of implied acts of sexual intercourse. Verbal references to intercourse increased from 2 to 53 a week during this time.

A rite of passage?

Other researchers and observers suggest modern American teenagers experiment with sex so casually because of changing social attitudes in recent decades. In this scenario, culture as a whole, by setting standards and expectations for sexual roles and behavior, determines people's

The increasing explicitness of sexual materials in the media, including TV, movies, videos, music CDs, magazines, and even clothing ads, is an often-cited theory for teenagers' openness about sexual matters. Here, two teenage boys check out a Victoria's Secret catalog.

sexual attitudes. This process of sexual role socialization, suggests sociologist Catherine S. Chilman, causes people of various genders, age groups, and economic levels to act in certain ways and fulfill certain roles, which are accepted by society as a whole. For example, she points out, young American women used to be routinely socialized to believe their major functions in life were childbearing, child care, and homemaking, and those who were considered decent young women did not have sex until they were married. Because society promoted this role so strongly, most teenage girls sought to fulfill it. Chilman continues:

> The late 1960s and the 1970s witnessed radical upheavals in the culture of sexuality. Sex-specific attitudes and behaviors became highly permissive, and the push for equal sex roles . . . became strong and widespread. In a sexually open and stimulating climate, young people . . . were almost forced to take a fairly public stand regarding their sexual identity.

In the absence of clear sexual guidelines and surrounded by growing sexual permissiveness, Chilman suggests, teenagers became increasingly casual about sex and more likely to act on their natural sexual urges. Another popular theory for why today's teenagers are so open and casual about their sexuality singles out changing family attitudes. According to this view, an increasing lack of parental guidance and supervision of young people has encouraged the idea that teens are more or less "on their own" in making important life decisions, including those pertaining to sex. "Teenagers who have spent huge blocks of their time either alone or with friends or taking care of siblings after school while their parents are at work," remarks writer Patricia Hersch, "have come to believe that they can handle anything. Anything," Hersch states, "includes being sexually active."

No single factor—explicit media depictions of sex, changing social attitudes, or lack of parental guidance—is in itself responsible for the more open and casual sexual attitudes of today's teenagers. All of these factors, along with others less obvious or talked about, are probably involved, and each factor tends to reinforce the effects of the others. Whatever the causes, no one doubts that many teens view becoming sexually active as a natural and expected rite of passage in the growing-up process; teens believe they themselves, not their parents, are the best judges of when they are ready to become sexually active.

Although teenagers most often cite a combination of curiosity about and readiness for sex as the reason they initiate sexual activity, they also cite other reasons. The second most frequently mentioned motive is love or a strong affection for a specific partner. From 10 to 25 percent of young men and from 30 to 50 percent of young women interviewed in various studies say they first had sex because they were in love. Other reasons include the desire to have a baby, a motive cited twice as often by girls than boys; the loss of virginity, either willingly or not, while under the influence of alcohol and/or drugs; and peer pressure. Peer pressure was cited in the "Sex in America" study as an important motive for becoming sexually active by as few as 3 percent and as many as 29 percent of the teenagers interviewed, depending on gender and other factors.

Peer pressure

Many adults seem surprised that peer pressure is not the single major motive for teen sexual activity. Politicians and educators of the 1980s and early 1990s certainly believed peer pressure was the chief culprit behind what they saw as an alarming rise in rates of teen sex. Operating on this mistaken assumption, some instituted school- and community-based programs, which rather narrowly targeted the effects of peer pressure among teenagers. One of the most notable examples was the program titled Education Now and Babies Later (ENABL), launched by Governor Pete Wilson of California in 1992. Designed to teach students between the ages of twelve and fourteen to resist pressure from their peers to become sexually active and thereby to reduce teenage pregnancy, the program's curriculum was completed by 312,000 teenagers statewide. But the program proved ineffective. A seventeen-month evaluation revealed no observable difference between pregnancy rates for ENABL students and those who had not taken the program. Wilson scrapped ENABL late in 1995, promising to replace it with something more effective.

No quick fix

The failure of the ENABL program underlines the pointlessness of trying to reduce the incidence of teen sexual activity by focusing on one isolated cause or factor. Although peer pressure is undoubtedly one cause, many others exist. All of the major causes teenagers cite, among them a feeling of readiness for sex, strong feelings of love, and the desire to have a baby, are firmly ingrained in the social and cultural fabric of American life. This makes trying to address any single cause without addressing other factors impractical, if not futile.

"Sexual practices can never be examined and understood independently of other social factors," says theologist Allen J. Moore. Sexual behavior, including that of teens, Moore maintains, is intertwined with issues ranging from the quality of teenagers' education about sex, which is often inadequate; to the economic level of parents, many of whom work long hours and leave children home alone, largely to raise themselves; to the ineffective policies and programs of politicians seeking a quick fix for

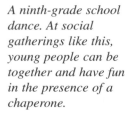

A ninth-grade school dance. At social gatherings like this, young people can be together and have fun in the presence of a chaperone.

sex-related social problems; to social stereotyping of gender and sex roles, a force affecting teens more strongly and more subtly than mere peer pressures. Explaining this social stereotyping, Moore writes:

> Young people today are socially pressured to be sexually active long before they have been prepared educationally and psychologically to cope with the deeply personal and highly charged nature of sexuality. . . . Our society's images of being male and being female demean the larger moral significance of sexuality. A teenage boy faces the social pressure to "score" and, in so doing, he reduces his partner to a sexual object. And a teenage girl absorbs the idea that a woman is someone who is sexually desirable to a man; her worth lies in her value as a sexual commodity and her ability to control the male with the sexual favors she provides.

Clearly, then, because teen sexual behavior is rooted in larger social and cultural trends and issues, effecting significant and lasting changes in that behavior will not be an easy or short-term process. Changes may require a concerted and long-term effort by parents, educators, politicians, health officials, religious leaders, and others to address the greater social issues and problems affecting children's lives and shaping their personal and sexual identities. Meanwhile, many teenagers and young adults continue to deal with the frequent consequences of being sexually active.

2

The Problems of Teenage Pregnancy and Parenthood

TEEN PREGNANCY AND its consequences consti-
tute one of the largest social problems in the United States
today. Each year more than a million teenage girls, an average of more than three thousand a day, become pregnant; of these, 65 to 70 percent are unmarried. By
comparison, only about 15 percent of adolescent women
who became pregnant in 1960 were unwed. Today, between 7 and 10 percent of pregnant teens have miscarriages that terminate their pregnancies, about 40 to 45
percent terminate their pregnancies by having abortions,
and about 50 percent go full term and have their babies.
Of those who do give birth, roughly 5 percent give up
their babies for adoption. This is a startlingly small figure
because in 1955, approximately 95 percent of all unmarried adolescents who carried their babies to term gave
them up for adoption. This means 95 percent of today's
teenage mothers—about half a million young women—
keep their babies. And a majority of them face daunting
and sometimes severe social, economic, and emotional
difficulties, including the interruption of education; the
need to pay for housing, medical bills, and child support;
the stress and exhaustion of caring for a baby; and the loss
of free time and a normal social life.

These difficulties are often shared by the boys who father the babies, young men who are typically as emotionally immature and unprepared for parenthood as the young mothers. Of course, not all teenage fathers accept their responsibility and stay with their partners. Some deny the babies are theirs and in other cases, the pregnant girls or their families reject the fathers' help or involvement for various reasons. Yet many young men do marry or live with their partners and babies so, like the young women, they face economic and social hardships and uncertain futures.

Each year, then, close to a million and a half adolescent girls and boys and their babies join the growing ranks of struggling families, many of whom become dependent on their own families or on government agencies for financial support. And parents, schools, and local, state, and federal government agencies continually examine the personal and social factors causing teen pregnancy and seek ways to reduce its incidence. According to Michael D. Resnick

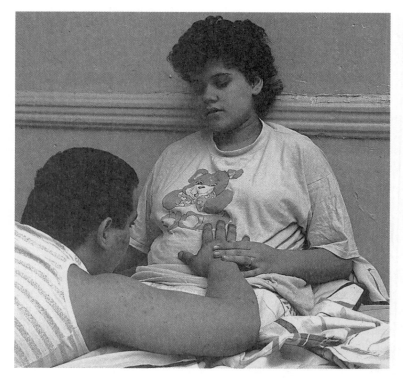

An eighteen-year-old father tries to feel the movement of his unborn child, carried by his seventeen-year-old girlfriend. Although they're just teenagers, these new parents now face adult responsibilities and uncertain futures.

of the School of Public Health, University of Minnesota, recent studies

> have documented high public expenditures associated with teenage pregnancy, rising levels of out-of-wedlock births, the contribution of [these] births to the creation and perpetuation of poverty in the U.S., and the connection between sexual activity and high rates of sexually transmitted diseases . . . among young people. As a result, teen pregnancy constitutes a high priority among social agencies, community organizations, and various levels of government.

Wanted versus unwanted pregnancies

The causes of teen pregnancy are many and varied. Although the vast majority of such pregnancies are unexpected and, at least initially, unwanted, a few are not only wanted, but consciously and purposely planned. Precise figures are lacking, but a growing number of adolescent girls, perhaps between 1 and 5 percent of those who become pregnant, most of them unwed, actually plan to have a baby and take on the responsibilities of parenthood. The reasons for making this life-altering choice vary. Some young women want to escape an abusive or emotionally difficult home life; others want a way out of a school environment where their grades are poor or they are experiencing social problems; still others say they want babies because they are looking for a relationship they currently lack and crave: someone to love, who loves them unconditionally in return. In Denver, Colorado, a pregnant high school senior recently told a local newspaper interviewer, "I wanted somebody to live for, something that would make me respect myself. I just wanted something to be mine, to take care of, someone to be there for me."

Some young men, too, purposely choose to become parents. In her book *Teenage Pregnancy*, Gisela Meier explains:

> Just as there are girls who intentionally become pregnant, there are boys who set out to become fathers. Generally, they are teenagers who are not doing well in school and live in impoverished communities where there are few jobs. Most of the families in their neighborhood survive on welfare. For

This nineteen-year-old college student is fortunate to have her boyfriend helping her raise their child. Many teenage mothers are single parents who must cope with the responsibilities and difficulties of raising children alone.

them, having a child is the one thing they can point to as an achievement. Some of them brag about how many babies they have fathered. Although these boys believe they are accomplishing something, they actually are making more difficulties for themselves and their girlfriends, not to mention the babies they are creating. There is a good chance their children will grow up with the same problems they had.

The young men and women involved in the majority of unplanned and unwanted pregnancies often face the same kinds of bleak economic and social consequences, and most of these, at least at first, suffer the added stress of feeling embarrassed, trapped, and hopeless. One major cause of such unwanted pregnancies is ignorance about sexuality in general, and about reproduction in particular. Despite the earnest efforts of some parents to inform their children and the existence of sex education classes in some schools, teenagers often learn about sex from their peers. In the latter case, not surprisingly, much exaggerated, misleading, and outright false information gets passed on. Many adolescents, for example, still believe the incredible myth that a young woman cannot get pregnant the first time she has intercourse. Other equally wrong myths say a girl will not get pregnant if she: has intercourse standing up, has sex extremely frequently, has sex extremely infrequently, has sex in a hot tub, jumps up and down after having sex, has sex during her period, douches with a soft drink after having sex, or has sex while drunk. Teens who believe such inaccurate stories have intercourse without using contraceptives and, more often than not, become pregnant.

All this ignorance about sex, coupled with the natural feeling of invulnerability characteristic of most young people, often produces a false sense of confidence about having sex—the "it can't happen to me" syndrome. Researcher Herma Silverstein describes a typical case of such denial:

> For most girls, finding out that they are pregnant comes as a shock, even if they have suspected it for some time. "It can't happen to me" or "There must be a mistake" are some common reactions to the news. Michelle was eighteen and about to graduate from high school when she became pregnant. "When the doctor told me my pregnancy test came out positive, I said, 'What do you mean it came out positive?' I walked out of his office in a kind of daze. It didn't really hit me until I was outside, and then I started crying and saying,

'Oh, my gosh. This can't happen to me.' I was walking down the street crying, and people were staring at me." When girls are as frightened as Michelle, they often do everything they can think of to hide their pregnancy. They almost seem to believe that if they don't think about being pregnant, the problem will go away. Some girls are able to postpone telling anyone for months.

School problems

Another factor influencing teenage pregnancy rates is consistently poor performance in school, what researchers call low educational expectancy. A number of studies have shown that young women and men who have low expectations about their education and what it can do for their futures are more likely to drop out and become young, and often unwed, parents. By contrast, most teenagers who see education as an important key to a better life tend to stay in school, avoid pregnancy, or, if they do get pregnant, get married. A report in *Family Planning Perspectives* states:

> Adolescents with high educational expectations are significantly less likely than others to become pregnant, and those who [do] become pregnant are significantly more likely than teenagers with low educational aspirations to have an abortion or to marry before the baby's birth.

Researchers have also found the effects of low educational expectancy cut across racial and ethnic lines and affect all kinds of teenagers more or less in the same ways. As Claire Brindis, pediatrics and health expert, points out:

> The High School and Beyond Study, looking at each ethnic group separately, found that white, black, and Hispanic sophomores with low academic ability [the lowest third of their class] were twice as likely to become unwed parents by their senior year as those students with greater academic ability. The National Longitudinal Survey of Youth found that females in the bottom 20 percent of basic reading and math skills were five times more likely to become mothers over a two-year period than those in the top 20 percent.

Researchers also suggest changing social attitudes have influenced teen pregnancy rates. For example, a few decades ago when a young, unmarried girl got pregnant, her pregnancy was considered shameful or even sinful.

This stigma is now much less prevalent and, in many cases, even nonexistent, so negative social pressure is no longer a credible deterrent to many teens having sex, getting pregnant, and giving birth. A national survey conducted in 1987 found only 23 percent of teenage women and men interviewed believed single women should never have children. In another survey, half the black female sophomores and one quarter of the whites responded they would, without reservation, consider having a child out of wedlock. As a result of such changing attitudes, the proportion of births outside of marriage has been rising in the United States for decades. One quarter of the American women who had babies in 1990 were not married and, overall, the country's unwed birthrate rose from just 5 percent of all reported births in 1960 to 27 percent in 1990.

Poverty

Experts also cite other causes for high rates of teen pregnancy. One cause is poverty, which often initiates a cycle of repeated behavior in succeeding generations. "Pregnant and parenting teens are far too often the offspring of educationally and financially disadvantaged single teenage mothers," report social workers LaWanda Ravoira and Andrew Cherry:

> For example, in the state of South Carolina in 1984, there were 1,964 babies born to black teens between the ages of 14 and 17, as compared to 465 infants born to white adolescents. Many of these youth [black and white alike] came from educationally and financially disadvantaged homes. They were the offspring of parents who themselves conceived during their teenage years.

Other causes behind the incidence of teen pregnancy include: becoming sexually active at a very young age (a girl's longer period of sexual activity increases her chances of getting pregnant); peer pressure, which has the strongest effect on boys and girls under the age of fifteen; the degree of closeness and trust between parents and teens (young people with poor parental relationships are more likely to end up parenting a child); and the degree of

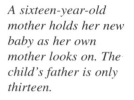

A sixteen-year-old mother holds her new baby as her own mother looks on. The child's father is only thirteen.

effective parental supervision of a teenager's dating activities and curfews.

Facing a very expensive future

The consequences of unplanned pregnancies for young women and men are always life altering. Of the nearly 40,000 teenage girls who leave school each year because they are pregnant, a large proportion never return. Teenage mothers are only half as likely to graduate from high school as girls who put off motherhood until their twenties, and only a small fraction of teenage mothers end up completing college. Teenage fathers fare no better. By the age of twenty, only four out of ten teenage fathers earn a high school diploma compared with nine out of ten of those teenage men who do not become fathers.

The impact of quitting school is usually profound. Teenage parents, both male and female, quickly learn that finding a good job and making a comfortable living is extremely difficult without a high school diploma. For many, the inability to find well-paying jobs is compounded by the increasingly high costs of raising children. In her book *Teen Pregnancy*, researcher Sonia Bowe-Gutman warns teens:

> If you become a parent, you are facing a very expensive future. It costs over $200,000 to raise a child until he or she is old enough to leave home. Day care costs a lot as well. You may not be able to find a job that pays you more than you spend to have your baby taken care of. Even when your child is in school, you will have to worry about summer vacations and year-round expenses for food, clothes, and toys.

The financial burden of raising children does not end with these expenses. Medical care for a normal, healthy baby now costs an average of $2,000 for its first year alone. If the child has health problems stemming from being born premature, underweight, or with permanent disabilities, all of which are more common for the infants of teenage mothers, medical care can become astronomical. Treating a low-weight baby during its first year, for example, averages $35,000.

The upshot of these financial considerations is that many young single mothers, either teenagers or older women who became pregnant as teenagers, cannot afford to make it on their own. They must depend on help from their families or from the government; the situation is similar in many instances in which the young father is present, but earns little money. Health officials estimate at least a third of all families started by teenagers receive some form of welfare aid, which is paid for by all American taxpayers. The most common forms of aid are Medicaid, which pays for child-related and other medical bills; Aid to Families with Dependent Children, which gives young mothers money for rent and living expenses; and/or food stamps, which help buy groceries. Overall, more than half the money the government spends on these three programs is paid out to teenage mothers or families begun by teenagers.

The emotional toll on teenage parents and their children is also great. Many teens have great difficulty coping with the enormous demands and responsibilities of parenthood. "I didn't know it would be like this," admits Jean, a seventeen-year-old single mother from Massachusetts, who is trying to raise her baby, work, and go to school at the same time. "I hardly see any of my friends anymore. Parties are out because I rarely can find a sitter and besides, I'm too tired the next day. . . . There's just day after day with long lists of stuff I have to do whether I like it or not." Angela, a nineteen-year-old single mother in California with two-year-old twin girls, echoes the same theme. "It's the stress," she says, rattling off the many duties and worries that go along with raising the children. "I love my babies, but I always wish I'd gotten an abortion or never gotten pregnant."

Teenage fathers experience similar difficulties adjusting to the strains and stresses of child-care responsibilities, sometimes well before the baby arrives. Gisela Meier cites the case of sixteen-year-old Paul, who dropped out of

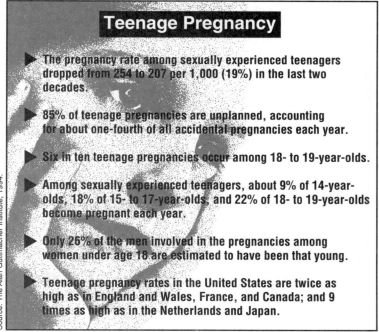

Source: The Alan Guttmacher Institute, 1994.

Teenage Pregnancy

► The pregnancy rate among sexually experienced teenagers dropped from 254 to 207 per 1,000 (19%) in the last two decades.

► 85% of teenage pregnancies are unplanned, accounting for about one-fourth of all accidental pregnancies each year.

► Six in ten teenage pregnancies occur among 18- to 19-year-olds.

► Among sexually experienced teenagers, about 9% of 14-year-olds, 18% of 15- to 17-year-olds, and 22% of 18- to 19-year-olds become pregnant each year.

► Only 26% of the men involved in the pregnancies among women under age 18 are estimated to have been that young.

► Teenage pregnancy rates in the United States are twice as high as in England and Wales, France, and Canada; and 9 times as high as in the Netherlands and Japan.

school to work full-time at a low-paying job, the only job he could find. Paul gives $40 to $50 a week to his girl-friend, also sixteen, to help cover the bills for her doctor visits. "I knew it was going to cut out a lot of my privileges and fun on the weekend," Paul says. "I knew it was going to cost me. I wish that I were older and that I had waited. The baby ain't even here, and already I have to pay."

Stress and frustration

With so many stresses and pressures, unfortunately some teenage parents take out their frustrations on their children. Neglect and physical abuse are common among families headed by teens and young adults, especially those experiencing the most severe economic difficulties and poorest living conditions. In addition, health care professionals observe, children born of very young and immature parents have a higher likelihood of suffering from emotional problems than those whose parents were in their twenties or older when their children were born. Meier says the children of most teenage parents "will probably not get a very good start in life, and they may grow up to repeat the mistakes of their parents. It's not difficult to see why many people consider teenage pregnancy to be one of the major problems facing our country."

Parents, health professionals, and government leaders would like to prevent as many of these unwanted pregnancies as possible. The trouble is not enough people agree about or have attempted widely and systematically to institute any one preventative approach. Proposals range from reforming welfare, either by increasing or eliminating government programs, depending on the approach; to increasing the quality of life and job opportunities for teenagers; and to taking a hard line and condemning and penalizing those young people who become pregnant and/or parent illegitimate children. Perhaps the most promising, easy-to-implement, and popular single approach, one already tested in some schools, is creating educational programs that increase teenagers' knowledge about sex and the serious consequences of unprotected sexual activity.

3

Sex Education: What Should Teens Learn?

ALMOST EVERYONE AGREES teenagers need education about human sexuality and the consequences of being sexually active. And little disagreement exists that such information should go beyond the basic facts of anatomy and biology, that is, the names and functions of the various reproductive organs. Teaching the basic facts of sexuality, a recent editorial in *Glamour* states, simply is not enough. "The facts increase knowledge but more intensive intervention [into teenagers' lives] is required to affect sexual behavior, experts have found. What *does* affect behavior is practical information. . . . And when you teach a teenager, you're also teaching the adult he or she will soon become."

In an age when more than a million teenage girls become pregnant each year, few people—liberal or conservative on the issue—can find fault with the basic premise of this editorial: Teens need to know, in advance, the possible consequences of their sexual behavior. Where controversy and debate do arise is about exactly what constitutes practical sexual information for teenagers and how far should the intervention of such information go into young peoples' lives. While a majority of people agree some kind of sex education is necessary for teens, many disagree, often strongly, about what specific sexual information must, or should, be taught.

Everyone at risk

Some agreement does exist about the information that should be taught in sex education: This agreement is mainly about character development and ethical attitudes. For example, no one argues with the idea of teaching teens they are responsible for their own actions, not only in sexual matters, but in all aspects of their lives. The more responsible young people are, one hopes, the less likely they will get into trouble. And everyone agrees teens should learn to respect others' needs, to have self-esteem, and to exercise restraint and self-control when they consider engaging in risky behavior.

Perhaps the only major point all sides agree upon in teaching the more specific and graphic aspects of sexuality is the need to warn teenagers about the dangers of STDs, including gonorrhea, chlamydia, genital herpes, genital warts, and HIV, among many others. Years ago, few people talked about diseases such as gonorrhea, often referred to as "the clap," partly because these diseases were not nearly as widespread as they are today. Also, many Americans viewed those who contracted such diseases as not worthy of mention in polite conversation.

Today, with between 55 and 60 million Americans infected and some 12 million new infections each year,

A ninth-grade health teacher confers with one of his students after class. Health classes are the most common setting for the presentation of sexual information in schools.

health officials recognize that everyone, regardless of their gender, race, or degree of morality, is at risk of catching STDs. Women are less likely than men to be tested for STDs, and they are more likely to suffer long-term complications such as infertility. Of women in general, health correspondent Hilary Kitasei points out:

> Teenage girls are at even greater risk than adults. An adolescent's cervix is more susceptible to infections of the lower reproductive tract, such as chlamydia. In addition, because teenagers have a higher rate of reinfection, they are more likely to experience long-term complications like infertility and ectopic pregnancy [implantation of the fertilized egg outside of the uterus]. Annually, three million teenagers contract STDs, and teenage girls have the highest rate of hospitalization in the U.S. for pelvic inflammatory disease (PID) caused by untreated chlamydia or gonorrhea.

Chlamydia and gonorrhea are, in fact, two of the most common STDs contracted by teens. Of the 3 million teenagers who get STDs each year, about a million suffer from chlamydia and approximately 250,000 from gonorrhea.

A need for more reliable information?

Other STDs are also increasingly widespread among teenagers. In the case of genital herpes only about 15,000 females ages fifteen to nineteen visited doctors and received treatment in 1966; by 1989 that number had risen to 125,000. And the number of doctor or clinic visits by teenagers of both genders for genital warts rose from an estimated 50,000 in 1966 to almost 300,000 in 1989. Health experts caution these figures represent only a small portion of the actual cases because most infected teens never go to a doctor. Some fail to report their STDs because they are ignorant of the symptoms and do not realize they have a serious infection, while others are too embarrassed to tell anyone. In general, say the experts, sexually active teenagers are two to three times more likely to get these common types of STDs than people age twenty or older, and they are far more likely to go untreated.

Of perhaps even more dangerous potential, many cases of HIV, which can lead to AIDS, may also go unreported

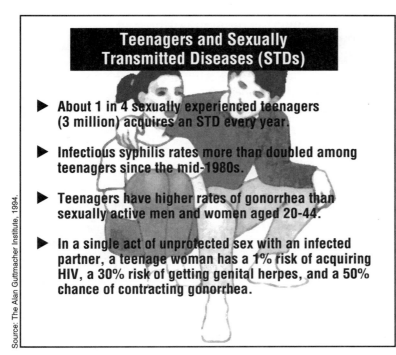

Source: The Alan Guttmacher Institute, 1994.

Teenagers and Sexually Transmitted Diseases (STDs)

▶ About 1 in 4 sexually experienced teenagers (3 million) acquires an STD every year.

▶ Infectious syphilis rates more than doubled among teenagers since the mid-1980s.

▶ Teenagers have higher rates of gonorrhea than sexually active men and women aged 20-44.

▶ In a single act of unprotected sex with an infected partner, a teenage woman has a 1% risk of acquiring HIV, a 30% risk of getting genital herpes, and a 50% chance of contracting gonorrhea.

and untreated. Ralph J. DiClemente, formerly with the Center of AIDS Prevention Studies at the University of California, San Francisco, writes:

> While the number of diagnosed cases of AIDS among adolescents remains relatively small compared with older age groups, ample cause for concern exists. Substantial . . . data describes the prevalence of high-risk behaviors among adolescents that increase the probability of HIV infection. Behaviors such as inconsistent condom use among sexually active adolescents, multiple sex partners, injection drug use, and the use of alcohol and other drugs that result in greater sexual [activity] are associated with greater likelihood of exposure to HIV.

The need for more reliable information about how STDs are contracted and their potential consequences, and for less embarrassment about discussing and seeking treatment for these diseases, was emphasized by the results of a recent study by the American Social Health Organization. When asked, "What is the biggest obstacle faced by people who want to protect themselves from STDs?" 25

percent responded "ignorance of how to protect themselves." About 16 percent said "lack of accurate information" was an obstacle, and some 45 percent cited embarrassment about discussing the subject. Important to note is the people interviewed in this study were adults. Health officials agree teenagers are far more likely to be both ignorant of the facts about STDs and fearful about revealing possible symptoms to others.

Negative results of teaching contraception

Some individuals and organizations advocate one way teenagers can avoid some of the risks of STDs is to use condoms, commonly called rubbers. Several U.S. government health organizations, for example, openly advocate condoms as an effective way to prevent sexually transmitted diseases. Using condoms and other contraceptive devices, advocates say, also greatly reduces the risk of pregnancy; they believe having teens learn about contraceptives and how to use them properly is very important.

Much less general agreement exists on teaching teens about using condoms and other types of birth control than about teaching them the dangers of STDs. Many of those opposed to teaching contraception believe such instruction actually encourages teenagers to experiment with sex and increases the incidence of teen pregnancies. Typical is a report first issued in 1986 by the Catholic Archdiocese of Boston, which states that the overall impact of teaching young people about birth control has merely been "that of further aggravating the problem of teenage pregnancy." More teens are using contraceptives, says the report, "and using them more consistently than ever before. Yet the rate of adolescent pregnancies continues to rise." The increased availability of birth control devices, the report continues,

> has only served to achieve the following: increased adolescent sexual activity; increased contraceptive use; increased contraceptive failure; increased teenage pregnancy; increased teenage abortion; increased teenage sexually transmitted diseases; [and a] decrease in the teen birth rate due to increased reliance on abortion.

The report strongly emphasizes rates of failure for contraceptive devices, making the point, for instance, that "for most [birth control] methods, women under 22 are about twice as likely to experience contraceptive failure as are those 30 and older."

Positive results of teaching contraception

By contrast, a number of recent studies endorsed by major medical and health authorities have produced evidence that seems to refute most of these arguments against teaching teenagers about birth control. Most other developed countries are very open about providing young people with information about contraception and the results are impressive. "European educators include contraception in family-life education throughout the middle and high school grades," comment researchers Linda A. Berne and Barbara K. Huberman:

In this scene from a school sex education class, the teacher holds up a diaphragm, one of the most commonly used contraceptive devices. Teaching about contraception is still a topic of heated debate.

> In a 36-country study [of pregnancy rates and sex education in industrialized nations, sponsored by the Alan Guttmacher Institute], it was found that, while girls in the United States initiated first intercourse at the same ages and with the same

frequencies as European girls, the rates of pregnancies were
two to seven times higher among U.S. girls.

Better knowledge and effective use of contraceptives also
contribute to lower rates of STDs among teenagers in
these countries. And because fewer of these teenagers get
pregnant, they have fewer abortions. This indicates that
sex education about birth control does not always or auto-
matically lead to the list of dire consequences cited by opponents.

Incorrect contraceptive use

Statistics also show the large failure rate of contraceptives used by teens in the United States, perhaps 12 to 40
percent, is, for the most part, not caused by the unreliabil-
ity of the products themselves (although no birth control
method is entirely foolproof), but by incorrect use. Many
who disapprove of teaching young people about contraception scoff at the idea that anyone must be taught how
to use condoms. Yet, sadly, many users—including some
married adults—make basic mistakes. According to Berne
and Huberman,"Some people who claim that they use
condoms for contraception don't use them every time, put
them on after they have had intercourse but prior to ejaculation, don't hold onto them during withdrawal, or use
petroleum-based lubricants that dissolve the latex." Supporting this contention, the Centers for Disease Control
and Prevention, the National Institutes of Health, and the
Food and Drug Administration have issued a joint report
that predicts a failure rate of less than 2 percent for the
consistently correct use of condoms.

Another common argument against teaching teenagers
about contraception is: They will then know how to avoid
the consequences of having sex and they will become
promiscuous or have sex very frequently with many different partners. But as William A. Fisher, a professor at the
University of Western Ontario, states:

> Several kinds of data have been adduced [cited] to show that
> this is *not* the case. First, Elizabeth Allgeier [a researcher
> from Bowling Green State University] noted that most

[American] teens have sex first, and seek contraceptive information later. Thus, sex education could help prevent unwanted pregnancies among the many teens who are already sexually active but who remain uninformed about contraception. Moreover, studies of teens who have obtained contraception show increases in frequency of intercourse [with the same partner], but *not* in the number of partners with whom they have sex.

In this example of the controversial process of "peer" education, a seventeen-year-old girl demonstrates the proper use of condoms to her male classmates.

Abstinence—a realistic goal?

Those who continue to oppose teaching about condom and other contraceptive use usually advocate the idea of counseling teenagers to abstain from having sex. The teaching of abstinence has itself become a controversial topic in recent years. Little doubt exists that a majority of adults would like to see teenagers refrain altogether from sexual activity or at least wait until marriage. Teenage abstinence on a massive national scale would certainly greatly reduce the incidence of pregnancies, abortions, and STDs among American teens. Working toward that end, many parents, teachers, doctors, and health care

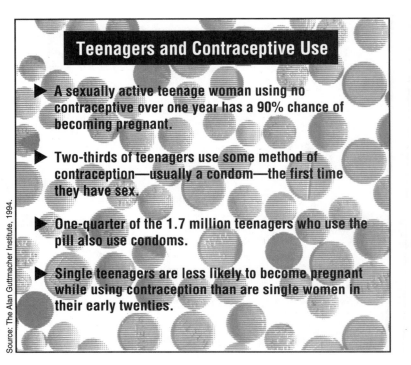

Teenagers and Contraceptive Use

▶ A sexually active teenage woman using no contraceptive over one year has a 90% chance of becoming pregnant.

▶ Two-thirds of teenagers use some method of contraception—usually a condom—the first time they have sex.

▶ One-quarter of the 1.7 million teenagers who use the pill also use condoms.

▶ Single teenagers are less likely to become pregnant while using contraception than are single women in their early twenties.

Source: The Alan Guttmacher Institute, 1994.

professionals advise teens to refrain from sex. A notable example is Michael D. Benson, physician and sex educator, who writes in his book *Coping with Birth Control*:

> This is the only method I endorse for teenagers. Simply stated, total abstinence means no sex. . . . Does no sex mean no kissing or hugging? What about petting? . . . For me, no sex means never having the penis inside the vagina or in contact with the vaginal opening. With this rule, total abstinence would be close to perfect in preventing pregnancy. Total abstinence has another benefit. Without genital-to-genital contact, the spread of a variety of diseases is almost impossible.

One question often asked about the teaching of abstinence is whether or not getting the vast majority of teens to abstain is a realistic, or even possible, goal and worth a systematic effort. Donald Macdonald, formerly of the U.S. Public Health Service, believes the effort is worthwhile, but that society hinders the effort by sending mixed messages:

> The behavior of adolescents is very much influenced by the messages conveyed in the attitudes and practices of those

around them, most especially their parents, peers, teachers, and the media that they hear and see. With regard to teenage sexual activity, abstinence is what we want from our children. Yet we often give ambivalent and confusing messages, as does the father who, while insisting that his daughter not engage in sex, urges her to use precautions if she must be active. Do we expect them to be abstinent, or don't we? When we seem willing to settle for less, we often get less.

Abstinence-only versus abstinence-plus

Macdonald's insistence that teaching abstinence should not be followed by teaching about birth control lies at the heart of the controversy surrounding this issue. No responsible educators or organizations are against the basic idea of urging teenagers to refrain from sex. What many individuals and groups do oppose is abstinence-only curricula, especially those that employ scare tactics to convey their message. "The focus on abstinence is not the issue," says Leslie Kantor of the Sex Information and Education Council of the United States:

> Rather, the abstinence-only curricula are problematic because of their reliance on instilling fear and shame in adolescents in order to discourage premarital sexual behavior. . . . Fear-based programs exaggerate the negative consequences of premarital sexuality and portray sexual behavior as universally dangerous and harmful.

Those who agree with Kantor say following up promotions of abstinence with information about responsible use of contraceptives is better. This is in the interest of helping those teens who end up becoming sexually active in spite of repeated urgings to avoid sexual activity. Supporting this view are studies of seven abstinence-plus programs in various states, which combined the two curricula. Students surveyed one to two years after completing these programs tended to refrain from sex longer than students in the control group (who were taught about abstinence only).

The question of which sexual topics teens should be taught and how is still open. Exactly who should teach teens about sexuality is also a topic of heated debate.

4

Sex Education: From Whom Should Teens Learn?

IN THE ONGOING debate over sex education, people are as divided about which individuals or groups should dispense sex-related curricula to teens as they are about the content of those curricula. Some believe sex education is strictly the province of parents and that strangers in schools and other organizations have no business forcing their opinions or personal agendas on children. Many others hold that parents, for various reasons, too often fail as sex educators, so the schools should provide teens with systematic, reliable information. Still others say churches and synagogues should play an important role in sex education. And, not surprisingly, some believe all these sources should play their part. Effective sex education, these people suggest, should be a broad-based, ongoing effort combining the talent and resources of parents, schools, and religious groups, as well as community-based programs and the media.

Whichever option is chosen or endorsed, a growing number of Americans accept that sex education of some kind should begin at an early age. They are increasingly worried about very young children being continually bombarded by sexually explicit images and ideas from television, movies, magazines, and their peers. A concerned educator concisely sums up the problem, saying, "Many

'Today, some of you will be leaving the hospital and going home to your families.
But, first, a lesson in sex education.'

of the five-year-olds I teach in my kindergarten class have
already been exposed to sexual images through the media.
Because of this, sex education *has* to start in elementary
school to put some of what these children see in perspec-
tive." Widespread agreement with this view came in a recent national magazine poll. Some 65 percent of those
surveyed said, regardless of who teaches about sex, such
teaching should begin by the time children reach elementary school; 29 percent said it should start when they are
in middle school. Only 1 percent thought young people
should wait until high school age to learn about sex. The
general consensus seems to be parents, teachers, or other in-
structors should gear information to the needs and abilities
of the specific age group; that is, for younger children the

information should be basic and general, and for teenagers sex education should be more detailed and specific.

Home-based sex education

This desire to tell teens only what they need to know only when they need to know it is precisely what makes a small but vocal minority of Americans feel parents alone should teach their children about sex. According to this view, dispensing such sensitive and potentially life-altering information is best left to parents, who know their own children better than anyone else and are, therefore, the best judges of what is appropriate for them to learn. "Parents, not the school system, should discuss sex with their children," one parent responded in a 1995 national poll on sex education. "It is not the place of bureaucratic institutions to be lecturing kids on something as personal and intimate as sexuality."

Tim LaHaye, author of several books on sex and marriage, agrees that parent-only sex education is the best

option. He places particular emphasis on the importance of parents instilling appropriate moral values along with sexual information. On the one hand, he recognizes the need for giving such information to all teenagers and even to pre-teens. "In the history of the world," he remarks, "it has never been more imperative that children gain information about sex at an early age." On the other hand, he warns that such information unsupported by parental values can lead to trouble.

> We can only be sure our children learn the essential facts together with moral values if we serve as the instructors ourselves. We must not leave this vital task to others, for in so doing we risk leaving our children vulnerable to sexual exploitation. In fact, we should assume in this sex-crazed day that our children will eventually be confronted with temptation. The only safeguard is parental preparation for that day. Most exploitation of children could be avoided by mental and moral training.

Few people argue with the idea that sex education should originate in the home. Indeed, various studies indicate teens who can and do converse openly with their parents about sex are much less likely to become sexually active at an early age. What bothers many researchers and educators who have closely studied or dealt firsthand with the subject is that in most American households no such open dialogue about sex exists. A majority of parents provide teenagers either with too little information about sex or with no information at all. According to Sol Gordon, a Syracuse University professor and noted expert on sex education:

> The idea that kids get information about sex from their parents is completely erroneous. Even the college-educated parents of my Syracuse University students offer very little. In survey after survey in a period of 12 years involving more than 8,000 students, fewer than 15 percent reported that they received a meaningful sex education from their parents. Usually girls were told about menstruation. The rest of the teaching could be summed up in one word: DON'T.

This situation usually results less from parental neglect or indifference than from lack of clear communication. Large numbers of parents, Gordon explains, themselves received

Teenagers clown around on their school playground. The question of whether schools should be a major source of sexual information for young people remains controversial.

little or no sex education as children. "Without one's parents to draw upon as a model, the cycle of noncommunication is repeated from generation to generation." Part of what perpetuates this communication gap, Gisela Meier suggests, is many well-meaning parents too easily accept one or more of the following common myths about their teenagers: "If they're not asking me any questions about sex, then they're not thinking about it"; "I know my son or daughter will come to me if he or she has a question or problem"; "If he or she were getting into trouble, I would know about it"; or "My kid doesn't want to listen to anything I have to say anyway."

Another problem is both parents and teens are often uncomfortable talking about sex with one another. Some parents are embarrassed to use explicit sexual terms around their children. Others avoid the subject because they have difficulty admitting their teenagers are sexual beings like themselves. And still others simply don't know where to start and how far to go on the subject of sexuality, so they end up continually putting off the talk. Many teenagers also have a hard time seeing their parents as sexual beings or they do not want their parents to know they are thinking about, considering, or actually having sex. So they, like their parents, try to avoid the subject.

With so many millions of parents and teenagers, even those with otherwise close relationships, failing to communicate about sex, it is easy to understand why a majority of both parents and students support the idea of an outside institution providing teens with sex education. Those few who favor churches and synagogues argue these institutions are already in the business of moral instruction. Why not have them go a step further and present a balanced combination of useful sexual information and values training? "With sex education," states one religious commentator,

> I think the church should take an active part in helping young people to foster the growth of a good value system. It is difficult for youth today to differentiate between the better things—doing what is normally and ethically right, and doing the pleasurable thing that "everybody else is doing."

Kenneth Guentert, a writer for the magazine *U.S. Catholic*, agrees religious institutions could be highly effective resources for teaching teens about sex, partly because they are already well organized and respected within communities. Using the Catholic Church as a specific example, Guentert points out:

> The church has the infrastructure [underlying organization, system, and facilities] that can make a difference. We have schools, CCD [religious instruction] programs, youth ministers and, most of all, parishes. The parish is accessible to families. They [parents and other adult relatives] can have some say in the kind of sex education that goes on there. They can even help teach—with very little in the way of formal qualifications.

The problem is, at least today, few churches have comprehensive, frank, or useful sex education programs. As a provider of sexual information to its children, Guentert admits, the Catholic Church "is doing very little to help parents in this area. That's too bad because the church vision of sexuality is good." Most other houses of worship in the United States, regardless of denomination, also remain untapped sources of effective sex education.

Schools try to fill the void

This leaves the outside institution—the schools—as the most commonly accepted potentially effective forum for teaching teens about sex. A few people remain vehemently opposed to school-based sex education programs. "Teaching sex education in mixed classes to hot-blooded teenagers without the benefit of moral values is like pouring gasoline on emotional fires," writes Tim LaHaye in his book, *Sex Education Is for the Family.* "An explosion is inevitable."

But many people disagree with this view. Much more prevalent is the opinion expressed by sixteen-year-old Rhonda:

> The high school I was at wouldn't permit sex education, because that would be promoting sex. That's not right. They think that if they teach about it, then that gives you a reason to go out and do it, because then you think you know about it. But a lot of kids are going out and doing it because they don't know about it.

Many parents and educators concur with Rhonda. They think schools can and should fill the obvious void of parental and church-based sexual instruction. They also believe, for teenagers, learning about sex should be an ongoing process, which includes input from parents at home and teachers at school, with each side supporting and reinforcing the efforts of the other.

Hundreds of school-based sex education curricula have been developed over the years in all parts of the United States. Most of these programs in the 1970s focused primarily on increasing factual knowledge about reproduction and emphasized the risk and consequences of creating unwanted pregnancies. A second generation of sex education curricula, beginning in the early 1980s, continued to focus on increasing knowledge, but placed more emphasis on clarifying values and developing decision-making and communication skills.

As sex researcher Douglas Kirby puts it, proponents of these programs "believed if students' values became more clear and their decision-making skills improved, they would be more likely to decide to avoid risk-taking behavior, and, if their communication skills improved, they would be more likely to communicate effectively their decisions to their partners." Later generations of sex educa-

A school health teacher listens to his students' questions about sexuality. Surveys estimate that less than 60 percent of American teens have received any sort of sexual information in school.

tion curricula have focused on specific goals, such as convincing teens to remain abstinent until marriage, or warning about and preventing the spread of HIV.

Results of studies of the effectiveness of these programs have been mixed. In general, most programs seem to have increased students' knowledge of reproduction and their awareness of the risks of sexual activity, at least in some small measure. A few studies suggest favorable progress. One study shows 22 percent of unwed girls who took sex education courses in school became pregnant, compared to 37 percent who did not take such courses. Yet many surveys found little or no difference in pregnancy rates for those who took sex education courses and those who did not; at least, none of these courses appear to have caused any *increased* rates of teenage sexual activity. At first glance, this may suggest school-based sex education, although not ineffective, has not been as effective as many of its proponents had hoped.

Yet many educators and sex researchers remain highly optimistic. They predict more substantial benefits will come over time. First, they say, sex education in American schools is still not widespread. Only twenty-three states actually require some sort of sex education in public schools, and counting those states and communities that have instituted programs voluntarily, no more than 60

This sex educator is discussing the meaning and importance of love in relationships between men and women. Some school sex education programs consider the emotional side of teenage relationships, while many others do not.

percent of girls and 52 percent of boys have taken sex education courses by age nineteen.

Most sex education courses are brief. Studies indicate only about 10 percent of students in the United States get forty or more hours of sex education in their entire school careers. All such programs remain largely experimental and differ widely in content, approach, and level of frankness. "My sex education," complains a woman now in her twenties, "was nothing but a film we saw in sixth grade that showed the female reproductive organs. That was it." Even today, no national agenda for sex education aims or content exists. Most sex education programs are uncoordinated and fail to teach students throughout their school years. "I doubt there are a dozen school districts [in the United States]," says Sol Gordon, "that have a kindergarten through 12th-grade sex-education program that even approaches those available in Sweden [widely recognized among the best in the world]."

Some innovative programs

Some experts see the possible great promise of school-based sex education in the experiences of a few outstanding, well-received programs. Such programs are thorough, frank, and unafraid to tackle controversial or sensitive issues; strongly stress values, responsibility, and respect for others, in addition to teaching the information; and give students firsthand contact with persons involved in the issues being discussed.

One common approach in these courses is to invite young mothers and fathers in their teens or early twenties to the class. These young parents tell their peers in their own language that having and raising babies at their age is not only uncool, but often a backbreaking and unrelenting struggle. With few exceptions, the students are absorbed and moved. They often ask tough questions and get eye-opening answers, as when teenage mothers visit classes in Fairfax County, Virginia, part of a highly respected family life curriculum overseen by educator Jerald Newberry. "While you're partying and going to dances," these young mothers typically tell students, "we're working two jobs and changing smelly diapers in between."

Newberry has reported similar positive results after inviting HIV-positive speakers into classrooms. "The kids will tell you," he says, "it's the best education they've had on any subject in high school." After hearing both male and female speakers with HIV, Newberry asked three senior girls for their reactions. "They could hardly speak," Newberry recalls. "One of them told me, 'I've had AIDS education since sixth grade, but this is the first time I've ever thought it could happen to me.'"

A teenage mother stands beside a list her sex education teacher has compiled of common difficulties and complaints experienced by teen parents. The teacher hopes to show other young women in the class that having a baby is not as glamorous and easy as many of them might suppose.

One short, but innovative, program in human sexuality taught at Barnstable High School in Massachusetts in the late 1970s, used similar tactics to great effect. This seniors-only course featured classroom visits by doctors and other experts who gave extremely frank presentations of topics like contraception and STDs. The course also included frequent sessions of role-playing, in which students, the teacher, and occasional guests improvised on real-life situations, ranging from a timid parent trying to tell a teenager the facts of life, to a boy attempting to talk his girlfriend into having sex, to a teenage girl anxiously informing her father she is pregnant. Often, students played adult roles and vice versa. Follow-up discussions explored the motivations of the characters, identified core moral values, and emphasized making responsible choices. Of the more than thirty students interviewed from ten to fifteen years after participating in the program, nearly all rated it as the most memorable, effective, and meaningful of their school experiences.

To be most effective, even model school programs like these must be augmented and supported by people and institutions the students know and trust, particularly parents. Teenagers, whose parents openly discuss and teach about sex, who then receive more information and support for sound values from schools, churches, or other community organizations, are the least likely to suffer the negative consequences of early sexual activity. As Sol Gordon aptly says:

> It's up to parents to make a start, whether they are comfortable with the subject or not. . . . We should at least teach teachers, psychologists, clergy, social workers and others who work with youngsters how to respond to young people's questions. We owe it to our children and their children to provide them with the information they need in a manner they will accept.

5

The Rise of School-Based Clinics

THE DEBATE OVER sex education and the continuing increase in the number of school-based sexuality programs have not been the only response to widespread alarm over rising rates of teen pregnancy in recent years. Concerned parents, educators, and community leaders have also begun to employ school-based health clinics. These facilities, usually located either within high schools or in separate buildings on high school campuses, are more comprehensive versions of nurses' offices, familiar in many American schools since the early 1900s. Like traditional school nurses, school-based clinics offer a wide variety of first aid and health services.

What makes school-based clinics controversial is, unlike school nurses, they also provide sex education information, tests for pregnancy and STDs, and birth control counseling and referrals. Some of these clinics go a step further and actually dispense contraceptives to teenagers. Some people see these sex-related services as necessary weapons in the battle against unwanted teen pregnancies; others say these services, especially handing out contraceptives, are extreme, unneeded, and actually promote, rather than discourage, irresponsible sexual behavior among teens.

A wide range of services

The first school-based health clinics appeared around 1970; they first gave out birth control devices in 1973. Since then, the number of these clinics has grown steadily. In 1990, more than two hundred were located in the United States, and by 1995, this number had increased to over five hundred. Funding for these facilities comes from a variety of sources, including the federal government, state, county, and city governments, and private organizations.

The rapid spread of school-based clinics indicates they serve specific needs in many communities. What exactly are these needs and how do school-based clinics attempt to address them? A 1994 report by the Ounce of Prevention Fund states:

> The school-based health center concept embraces the idea that many childhood health problems have complex psychological, social, and physiological [biological] roots and that effective solutions will reflect this complexity. . . . School-based health centers supply adolescents with access to resources that they may otherwise lack. Often teens have only rudimentary knowledge of preventive medicine and nutrition. Doctors and hospitals are scarce in many urban neighborhoods and rural areas. Many teens do not have insurance coverage for the [health] services they may need. Many also lack caring relationships with adults who encourage healthy behavior. . . . Health centers are a core component of strategies to reach at-risk teenagers with a variety of social services.

Specific services vary from one school-based clinic to another, but among the most common are physical exams, nutrition facts and programs, mental health counseling, sports physicals, immunizations, treatment of eating disorders, weight management programs, vision screening, treatment of injuries, and substance abuse education. Much of what makes these clinics popular, useful, and, in some areas, essential is they provide vital general health services locally to many adolescents who would normally be unable to find and/or afford them.

If only these services were provided by school-based clinics, probably no one would oppose their presence in or near schools. The opposition invariably comes from the sex education and related services the majority of these clinics offer to teens. A brief examination of three successful Chicago school-based clinics reveals the nature of some of these services and how they are typically implemented. The program Toward Teen Health opened school health centers at Jean Baptiste Point DuSable High School in 1985, Rezin Orr Community Academy High School in 1986, and the Richard T. Crane High School in 1987. All three schools are located in economically depressed neighborhoods.

By the halfway point of the 1993–1994 school year, about 3,000 students, representing over 80 percent of the total combined enrollment of the three Chicago schools, had voluntarily registered to receive services at these health clinics. Of the more than 2,000 student visits to the clinics recorded in that half-year, about one-third were related to reproductive health and family planning. Clinic personnel dispensed information on sexuality and birth control and conducted several pregnancy tests. Because low birthweight (less than five-and-a-half pounds) is the

This nurse-practitioner helps run an adolescent health center in a large Illinois high school. Illinois maintains a network of school-based health clinics.

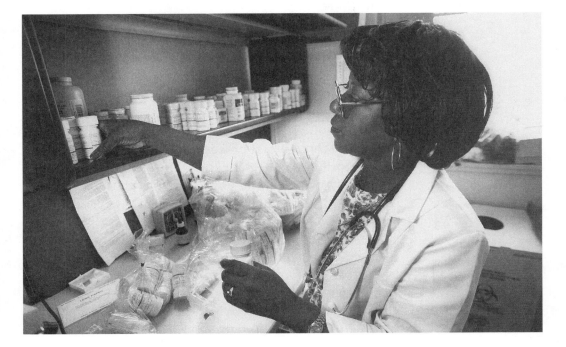

leading cause of infant death in the nation, they also set an agenda that places special emphasis on combating low birthweight in babies born of teenage mothers in the area. In addition to regular pregnancy testing, clinic services, such as prenatal care and nutrition programs, and prenatal support groups, combined efforts to improve the likelihood for teen mothers to deliver healthy babies. During this same half-year, the clinics also tested about 500 students for STDs and successfully treated 157 of them.

Do clinics help reduce teen pregnancy?

School-based clinics, like those of Chicago's Toward Teen Health program, are obviously effective in their care of teen mothers, application of preventive medicine, and treatment of specific diseases and ailments. But are these kinds of facilities effective in reducing the incidence of teen pregnancy? This is a question often asked by opponents of school-based clinics, who worry that these clinics, particularly those teaching about and dispensing birth control, might actually contribute to *increases* in teen pregnancy by encouraging sexual activity, and even promiscuity in teens. Roger Mahony, archbishop of Los Angeles, has frequently voiced this concern. "By making contraceptives readily available," he says, "the clinics' personnel will tacitly promote sexual relations outside of marriage for boys and girls, many of whom are barely in their teens."

No comprehensive nationwide studies have been done to date on the overall effectiveness of sex-related programs in school-based clinics. Studies conducted have either concentrated on individual schools or local regions, or they have evaluated the clinics on overall health care. A 1991 study, for instance, issued the rather general and inconclusive finding that school-based clinics "provide accessible, affordable health care to poor children [and] may also be an effective means of reducing rates of teen pregnancies and improving birth control outcomes for young women who do become pregnant."

The results of a well-known study of a clinical program based in Baltimore, Maryland, in the 1980s were a bit more specific. According to physician and medical researcher Laurie Zabin, who helped evaluate the program, the health facility was

> designed and administered by the staff of the Johns Hopkins School of Medicine's Department of Pediatrics and Department of Gynecology and Obstetrics. The project was carried out with the cooperation of the administrators of four schools in the Baltimore school system—two junior high schools and two senior high schools. The program provided the students attending one of the junior high schools and one of the senior high schools with sexuality and contraceptive education, individual and group counseling, and medical and contraceptive services over a period of almost three school years. Students in the remaining two schools received no such services . . . and served as the control sample.

The study that eventually evaluated the program found these sex education and related services did not encourage more sexual activity among the students who received them. Also recorded were higher rates of condom use, ostensibly because of easier accessibility to these devices, which produced a slightly lower teen pregnancy rate. Describing another important result of the clinic program, Zabin says:

> It appears to have encouraged the younger sexually active teenagers to develop levels of knowledge and patterns of behavior usually associated only with older adolescents. This accelerated protective behavior, coupled with evidence that first coitus [intercourse] was not encouraged but, in fact, postponed, should provide solid support to the current movement toward the introduction of school-based clinics.

A school-based clinic instituted in a St. Paul, Minnesota, high school produced similar data. Researchers found that birthrates among students who used the clinic dropped by one-half over a period of a few years.

Opponents voice their concerns

Opponents of school-based clinics, including a number of religious leaders, school-board members, school administrators, parents, and a few health care providers, remain unconvinced by these cases. Stan Weed, of the Institute for

Research and Evaluation in Salt Lake City, for example, calls the results of the Baltimore study "questionable." The size of the sampling of pregnant girls was very small, he points out, and the behaviors of these teenagers may not reflect the behaviors of girls across the nation. Furthermore, the Baltimore case, even if moderately successful, says Weed, may represent merely an isolated case. After conducting his own investigation of the effectiveness of school-based clinics' sexuality programs, Weed concluded such programs are counterproductive. Despite the increasing presence of these clinics in the United States in the 1970s and 1980s, he says, national pregnancy rates continued to rise.

Opponents of sex-related services at school-based clinics voice their doubts. One important concern is whether offering such services to teens might be undermining parental authority, thereby distancing many adolescents from their parents. If so, these young people might receive much less exposure to their parents' traditional moral and religious values. According to Roger Mahony:

> Parental values will influence most teens, and educating young people to morally responsible views of sexual relationships, as designed by God for the covenant of marriage, is a priority for most parents. However, school birth control clinics send a message to students legitimizing behavior contradicting our Judaeo-Christian ethic. Their intrusion into public school education interferes with the rights of parents and their children to the free exercise of religious values. Teens [who use these clinics] will be able to make serious health decisions concerning the use of oral contraceptives, treatment of sexually transmitted diseases, and abortion without parental involvement, and we will see the legitimate role of parents being undermined. It is no wonder William Bennett, the U.S. Secretary of Education [under President Ronald Reagan], said, "Such clinics open up the possibility of a wedge being driven between students and those who should have the greatest influence on them—their parents."

Widespread support

Those who support school-based clinics see no such wedge being driven between parents and teenagers to date. Some proponents point out that many of the adolescents who use these clinics come from impoverished areas, where broken and single-parent homes are common and parental guidance is already largely lacking. A majority of the pregnant girls who frequent big-city school-based clinics report that their parents physically or sexually abuse them, or suffer from alcoholism or drug addiction. Desperate for love and guidance, these young people naturally develop close relationships with some adults who work in the clinics. The clinical staff find they spend much of their time providing emotional support. Clinic supporters contend these kinds of out-of-family friendships instill such values as self-esteem and personal responsibility in teens without role models for these values at home.

This and other perceived positive benefits of school-based clinics have struck a chord with Americans of all walks of life. Despite the concerns of some vocal opponents like Mahony and Bennett, a significant majority of adults in the United States support such facilities, including those that provide birth control information and contraceptive devices. A 1991 Roper Organization poll found that 64 percent of American adults support the idea of schools dispensing contraceptives. A similar *Time* magazine poll found 84 percent of adults in favor of the idea. In addition, a Lou Harris Poll found that 67 percent of adults think establishing, or linking up with, school-based clinics should be mandatory for schools: In Michigan, 80 percent of those polled in a statewide survey said they supported school health centers that provide students with confidential information; in similar surveys conducted in Portland, Oregon, and San Francisco, California, the concept of such centers received 77 percent and 93 percent support rates, respectively.

"They've helped my kids"

One such school-based clinic supporter is Cathy, a Boston mother of two teenagers—a fourteen-year-old boy and a sixteen-year-old girl. Both teens are sexually active and have received birth control information and devices from their local school clinic. Cathy believes teenagers having sex is a fact of life and that school-based clinics are one way to keep this activity under control. "I got pregnant myself when I was just a kid," she says.

> In those days there weren't any sex-ed classes or health clinics in the schools in my area. Mostly you couldn't talk to your folks about sex, so you were pretty much on your own when it came to learning the score. Like a lot of my friends, I made the mistake of having sex too early and didn't know a damn thing about birth control. Look where it got me—pregnant and a school dropout. . . . Well, my own kids are having sex too young, too, no matter how much I've drummed it into them not to. But what I did do was take them over to the [school] clinic and we all sat down and talked to the counselors together. Their [the teenagers'] attitudes are much bet-

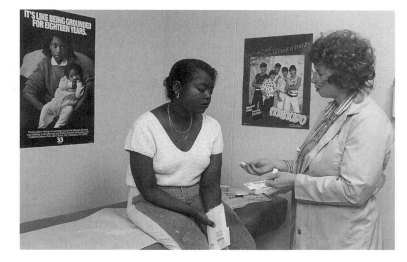

A nurse discusses birth control methods with a student at a high school health clinic in Dallas, Texas.

ter now and they know they're the ones responsible for their actions. . . . I go over [to the clinic] a couple times a week now, along with other mothers from my area, and talk to the kids and tell them the score. What the hell. These clinics aren't the be-all and end-all. But they've helped my kids stay in school and stay out of trouble.

The Ounce of Prevention Fund's 1994 report echoes this same theme: Although school-based clinics cannot solve the serious social and health problems many communities and schools now face, they *can* make a positive difference in the lives of some teens. This report states:

Depending on geographic location, adolescent health may encompass the effects of poverty, violence, racism, limited future options, drugs, and peer pressure. . . . While school-based health centers cannot cure [these] socioeconomic and environmental ills, they can help students cope more effectively with them.

6

Changing Attitudes About Gay Teens

THE TOPIC OF homosexuality has been widely discussed in the media in recent years for two reasons: first, because gay activists demonstrate for equal rights and, second, because of increased scientific research into its causes. Yet one aspect of homosexuality—its occurrence in teenagers—is not often discussed. This may be because many people, including large numbers of teenagers, mistakenly assume homosexuality in teens is rare and too few gay teens exist to make this a worthy topic of conversation. Another reason gay teens are rarely discussed is many people find this topic disturbing and feel uncomfortable talking about it.

How many teenagers are gay? No one knows for certain. Researchers say the proportion of gay, lesbian, and bisexual teens to straight teens is probably similar to the proportion of gay people in the general population. The most commonly accepted and cited figure is 10 percent, although this remains no more than a guess. Some recent studies have suggested a smaller figure. The "Sex in America" study, for example, produced an estimate of 3 to 5 percent for men and perhaps half that for women, although interviewers in this study did ask questions such as "Do you consider yourself homosexual?" or "Have you had sex with someone of the same gender?" which may

have limited honest responses. Because of widespread ho-mophobia, or fear and hatred of homosexuals, and the shame and rejection often accompanying the admission of being gay, many gay people may choose not to reveal their sexual orientation in such surveys. If existing estimates are used, a safe guesstimate may be: In an average high school of 2,500 students, as few as 50 or 60, or as many as 250, are gay.

Whatever their numbers, teens who know or suspect they are gay and are trying to cope with these feelings, in-variably find they must also find some way to deal with society's frequently hostile attitude toward homosexuality. "Schools typically are 'hostile' environments for gay and lesbian youth," says Barbara Rienzo, of the University of Florida's Department of Health Science Education. "School personnel are often not prepared to address sexual orientation issues and often have a negative bias toward gay and lesbian youth. Their peers share this bias and pro-vide very strong motivation for gay . . . students not to dis-close their identity." Fearing humiliation, rejection, or even physical violence, most gay teens learn to hide their sexual identity quietly, or to stay in the closet. Most re-searchers believe the vast majority of gay teens remain in the closet for the rest of their lives. At the same time, many straight teens, unaware of the sexual orientation and emotional plight of some of their gay classmates, remain

A gay pride parade in San Francisco. Although such public demonstations have become increasingly common across the country, the vast majority of gay people, young and old alike, keep their sexual orientation a secret.

homophobic as they grow older. So during the teenage years, most people, gay or straight, first confront and develop lasting attitudes about the issue of homosexuality.

What does being gay mean?

Whether open or secretive about their sexual orientation, most gay teenagers who realize they are homosexual (some teens are unaware of this until they are older) naturally wonder why they are gay. Many agonize over it, reasoning that if they could pinpoint the cause they could change and be like their straight friends. Unfortunately, no one knows for certain what causes homosexuality. A number of recent scientific studies do suggest various biological and genetic factors may be involved. One group of researchers, for instance, reported in 1991 that a specific brain region is two to three times smaller in homosexual men than in heterosexual men. In 1993, scientists at the National Cancer Institute discovered the first evidence for the existence of a gene that helps determine sexual orientation. The same researchers announced even stronger evidence for a "gay gene" in the journal *Nature Genetics* in 1995.

These and other similar findings do not necessarily indicate that homosexuality is strictly hereditary. Many researchers suspect sociological factors—such as home environment, methods of nurturing, and types of early physical and learning experiences—may also help determine whether a person becomes gay or straight (although exactly which factors are involved and to what degree remains unknown). Overall, most scientists presently believe homosexuality results from an undetermined and very complex mix of genetic and sociological factors, which may differ from one culture and even from one individual to another.

This strongly indicates homosexuals, whether teenagers or adults, do not consciously choose or decide to be gay, something gay people have insisted upon all along. "People think homosexuality is . . . a choice. It's not," says Gordon, a gay seventeen-year-old who has experienced much harassment and abuse from straight classmates. "It's not like I woke up and said, 'Oh, I think I'll be gay today,' like I think I'll wear my blue jeans today. If it was a choice, I would have chosen to be straight."

Gay teens frequently say, even before they realized they were gay, they knew they were somehow different. In a recent survey conducted by the University of Minnesota Youth and AIDS Project, educators Leo Treadway and John Yoakam report, "gay male adolescents interviewed . . . remembered this awareness of difference from peers as occurring between ages 5–7, or about the time they entered school. Neither they nor their parents initially connected this awareness with anything related to sexuality." Richard, now seventeen, remembers feeling different at about the age of eight or nine. "When we [the boys] were little," he says, "we thought girls were disgusting, but when the rest of my friends changed their minds and started to like girls, I didn't."

Only when Richard grew older and realized he was actually attracted to other boys, did he realize what this feeling of being different was really about. When Richard heard his friends and some adults use homophobic names, such as queers and fags, and say homosexuals are sick and perverted, he realized society believes it is not okay to be gay. Like all young homosexuals, Richard heard some

Many teenagers who have strong sexual attractions for members of their own gender deny they are gay, or hope they are not, because they see how badly society often treats gay people.

people say gays choose to be that way, but Richard knew better. His only real choice was whether he should reveal his feelings to others or keep those feelings hidden. He eventually told a guidance counselor and his parents, all of whom were sympathetic and understanding.

Many negative stereotypes

Not all young gays and lesbians are as fortunate as Richard. Many of those who do come out, wish they had not. Take the case of Jerry: At age sixteen, Jerry also admitted his sexual orientation to a guidance counselor, who "did not react favorably at all. He had no idea what to do—he acted like this was something he would have to go research." When Jerry told his parents, they kicked him out of the house and refused to speak to him for over a year.

The reactions of Jerry's counselor and parents to the news he is gay are not uncommon. Many people are so conditioned by negative stereotypes about gays, most of them erroneous, they cannot, at first, see past their homophobia. The mistaken idea that homosexuality is a conscious choice is only one of many myths children and teenagers hear; then from ignorance, they accept and perpetuate these myths into their adult years. Even many gay teens, who lack the facts themselves, may believe some of the negative stereotyping and lapse into self-hatred.

The level of ignorance and misunderstanding pervading society about homosexuality was clearly revealed in the outcome of learning exercises conducted in the experimental Barnstable High School sexuality program. The teacher began the first lesson on the topic by writing several dozen common beliefs about gays on the chalkboard. Among these were "gay men cannot control their sexual urges," "lesbians all have deep voices and dress and act like men," and "gay people actively recruit or try to convert straight people to become gay." The teacher then went through the items on the list, one by one, asking students to rate whether or not they thought the statements were "always true," "sometimes true," or "always false." In class after class, year after year, the results were the same.

Students identified over 80 percent of the statements either as always or sometimes true. When, at the end of the class period, the teacher revealed all the statements were either false or often false, the students typically expressed shock and disbelief. (In the following two days, the teacher followed up by presenting the results of studies showing that the popular stereotypes are often wrong.)

With so much ignorance and misunderstanding concerning homosexuality, it is no wonder that so many gay teenagers choose, out of fear, to hide their true feelings. Treadway and Yoakam say many gay teens

> submerge themselves into the general school population. They deliberately wish to go unnoticed so peers, teachers, and parents will not suspect the "secret" of their sexual orientation. Many young gay men and lesbians date members of the opposite gender to appear unquestionably heterosexual. In fact, some lesbians become pregnant and some gay males father children as if to confirm their heterosexuality. Such behavior would appear to remove any doubts from the minds of friends or family members who might suspect them as gay or lesbian.

Also not surprising are those gay teenagers who keep their sexual orientation secret, typically feel isolated, rejected, and increasingly frustrated. This makes them more vulnerable than their straight peers to problems with drug abuse, alcoholism, truancy and dropping out of school, and even suicide. The Institute for the Protection of Gay Youth, an educational and advocacy group for teenagers and young adults in New York City, which sees more than one thousand clients each year, reports that 21 percent of these young men and women attempt suicide before they reach the age of twenty.

Changing times

On a more positive note, the atmosphere for gay teens, traditionally one of isolation, rejection, and hostility, appears to be slowly improving. First, in the past twenty years, the medical community, after numerous studies and evaluations, has concluded homosexuality is not a sickness or an abnormal condition. The American Psychiatric

Gay teens at a demonstration. Organized demands by gay people for fair treatment and an end to homophobia have become increasingly common in recent years.

Association, American Medical Association, American Psychological Association, and American Nurses' Association all now recognize that in each succeeding generation, a small minority can be expected to be gay. Analogies have been made to the minority of people in each generation who are left-handed, as compared to the majority who are right-handed.

Second, adult gay activists have become increasingly vocal and organized in recent years. Through public demonstrations, appearances on TV and radio talk shows, literature, and educational talks and seminars, they have promoted, and sometimes even demanded, more understanding and better treatment of gays and lesbians. They explain that because of their youth and immaturity, gay teens who suffer homophobic abuse are particularly at risk for depression and suicide; they need to grow up in a more tolerant environment. According to John D. Anderson, a Stratford, Connecticut, high school teacher and recognized authority on gay issues:

Twenty-five years of hard work by countless people [gay activists and understanding straight supporters] have yielded
the best environment for lesbians and gays in our country's
history. For the first time, an American president [Bill Clin-
ton] has publicly said the "g word" and has even appointed
an open lesbian as assistant secretary of the Department of
Housing and Urban Development [Roberta Achtenberg, who
later resigned to pursue elective office].

Achtenberg's appointment highlights another change in
society, which has begun to benefit gay teenagers trying to
understand their identities and to develop personal self-
esteem. Many well-known, respected, and highly admired
people have freely admitted they are gay, creating positive
role models young gays can identify with and emulate.
Over one hundred highly placed U.S. government officials
and legislators are openly gay, including Congressmen
Barney Frank and Gerry Studds, both of Massachusetts.
Other gay role models include world-class tennis player
Martina Navratilova, 1984 Olympic gold medalist Bruce
Hayes, pop singers k.d. lang, Melissa Etheridge, and Elton
John, and poet Adrienne Rich.

The role of education

Education has been another area of change. The National Education Association and American Federation of
Teachers have both endorsed fair, humane, and equal treatment of gay and lesbian teenagers. The National Education Association's Division of Human and Civil Rights
recommends that educators respect the confidentiality of
students who confide their homosexual orientation or who
ask for assistance in this matter. It also recommends that
school personnel intervene to stop harassment, including
name-calling of gay and lesbian students, and promote in-
service programs to help teachers and counselors deal effectively with gay and lesbian youth. Actually
implementing these goals on a large scale is much more
difficult than merely recommending them. Many schools
still exclude the topic of homosexuality from sex education curricula and refuse to allow open discussions about
gay issues.

Yet an increasing number of school curricula and programs do address these issues and the needs of gay students. An outstanding example is Project 10, originally begun in 1984 as a prevention program for gay school dropouts by educator Virginia Uribe at Fairfax High School in Los Angeles. Over the years, the program has greatly expanded and now includes teacher training, counseling for students, and discussions of gay issues in classrooms. Such discussions often make fearful and confused gay students realize they are not alone, as in the case of Greg, who graduated from Fairfax High in 1988. "Being associated with Project 10," Greg says, "has given me the chance to articulate the needs of a silent minority. . . . I no longer consider myself stigmatized or different from other students." Praising Uribe's program, Mitzi Henderson, president of Parents, Families and Friends of Lesbians and Gays, based in Washington, D.C., states, "Project 10 has been invaluable. It has raised awareness of how issues confronting gay and lesbian students lead to high risk for truancy, dropping out, substance abuse, and suicide."

A scene from a gay and lesbian senior prom sponsored by the Los Angeles School District. Gay teens say they deserve access to the same avenues of social expression enjoyed by straight teens.

Educators like John Anderson point out the need for more programs similar to Project 10. To combat the negative and hurtful effects of homophobia, he advocates, school teachers, administrators, and especially guidance counselors and psychologists, need to educate themselves about homosexuality. Anderson also recommends classroom programs to teach students about the subject. This suggestion provokes controversy, however, for many people disapprove of the idea of schools teaching about homosexuality. Some feel such instruction is an attempt to indoctrinate students with ideas about being gay. Others are uncomfortable about young people being exposed to information about gay issues because their religion condemns homosexuality. Anderson suggests classroom instruction need not promote or endorse homosexuality. Such programs can make students aware of major gay issues and the debates surrounding them, and direct students toward factual information. At the very least, says Anderson, schools can and should provide a safe and tolerant learning environment for all students, including those who are gay.

Epilogue

A Word on the Accuracy of Sexual Surveys and Studies

A GROWING NUMBER of social, health, government, and private organizations periodically conduct surveys and studies of teenage sexual activity, some of which are discussed and quoted in this book. The first well-known and influential such study, conducted by the researcher Alfred Kinsey in the 1940s, examined teen sex as part of the larger and more general context of sexual behavior in America. Later, government health organizations, most notably the CDC, as well as private organizations, began conducting studies and regularly compiling statistics on sexual practices, including those of teenagers. Some of the more important recent studies of teen sex include: the National Survey of Family Growth, conducted periodically since 1982; the National Survey of Adolescent Males, conducted periodically since 1988; the Youth Risk Behavior Survey, conducted periodically by CDC; and the controversial study conducted at the National Opinion Research Center at the University of Chicago, the results of which were published in the 1994 book, *Sex in America: A Definitive Survey.*

Important to note is that the data collected and conclusions drawn by these and other studies are not definitive, complete, foolproof, or wholly accurate, as those who conduct these surveys readily admit. Results from any two studies on the same topic can be and often are inconsis-

tent, vague, or even contradictory. This can leave the public wondering which study to believe, and this belief factor is central to whether or not the results of a study are taken seriously. People tend to have preconceived notions about sexual behavior, even before examining such surveys; these views are molded by individual experiences and/or social stereotypes. If the results of a particular study contradict their preconceived ideas, many people will view the results as suspicious. They will dismiss or ignore them, no matter how much the researchers defend their accuracy and lack of bias.

For example, Joseph Adelson, professor of psychology, University of Michigan, tells about when he was teaching a seminar on the troubles of adolescence to college freshmen, he mentioned a statistic reported in the recently published book, *Sex in America*. According to this study, the average American woman has only two sexual partners in her lifetime. "The reaction in my classroom," recalls Adelson

Teenagers respond to a sex survey. The idea of asking young people sexually explicit questions is controversial and often affects the way such questions are phrased.

was electric—amazement, disbelief. That can't be! It's more than that! They must be lying! These are youngsters . . . who can absorb the most horrendous social statistics—that the killing of adolescents has increased fourfold in the last decade, that two-thirds of all black children are born out of wedlock—without batting an eye. They may or may not find such data troubling . . . but they do not find them shocking. What shocked them was the *not*-shocking—news of modesty, decorum, restraint.

Apparently based on their own teenage experiences, Adelson's students believed most women have more than two sexual partners in their teenage years alone.

A number of factors contribute to the difficulty of finding data on teen sex that is simultaneously accurate, consistent, and believable to a majority of people. First, conducting sexual surveys is expensive; in the mid-1990s, the cost of interviewing one participant (counting salaries of interviewers; fee, if any, to interviewee; office, lab, transportation, and computer costs; and other expenditures) was about $450 to $500. This severely limits the number of people who can be interviewed in any one study to a few thousand at most. Some critics question the reliability of such limited studies. They say to make so small a sampling of people unbiased and reflective of society as a whole is difficult, if not impossible.

A controversial undertaking

Another problem is, historically speaking, the idea of adult researchers asking personal sexual questions of teenagers has always been controversial. Some people continue to maintain interviews they consider so provocative only encourage and legitimize sexual experimentation by the teens. "As with drug use and alcohol consumption," comment behavioral scientists Susan Newcomer and Wendy Baldwin, "researchers have been asked if inquiring about sexual activity may have the unintended effect of increasing such activity. While no sound study has ever demonstrated such an effect, the concern remains." As a result, many researchers continue to interview only selected groups of teenagers or to ask a limited range of questions. Critics have legitimate grounds for calling such surveys incomplete and slanted, and for questioning the accuracy of their conclusions.

Even when the important relevant questions do get asked, other factors can affect the accuracy of the data. First, as in interviews of any kind, the participants can, and sometimes do, lie or exaggerate, as is often the case with young men who try to appear more sexually experienced than they are. According to Douglas Besharov, a scholar at the American Enterprise Institute in Washington, D.C., "One should always take young males' reports about their sexual exploits with a grain of salt."

Even when young interviewees are trying to be as truthful as possible, they can sometimes mislead researchers out of ignorance. When asked whether or not they have had sexual intercourse, for instance, many young girls who have been raped say yes, but they do not mention the rape itself. Some researchers estimate the initial sexual experience of as many as 7 percent of young people may be involuntary, and when such experiences are inadvertently lumped together with voluntary sex, the data and conclusions of a study can be slanted and partially invalidated. Similarly, some young teens, unaware that the interviewers define sexual intercourse strictly as penetration of the vagina by the penis, report having had intercourse when they have not. In a two-year follow-up of one study, for example, a young woman admitted, "Last time I told you that I had sex, but I really hadn't, and now I have and know that what I did before wasn't intercourse."

The upshot of these and other similar factors is not that most studies are misleading and worthless, but that even the largest and most carefully conducted surveys are imperfect and not to be taken literally. Besharov offers a useful rule-of-thumb for weighing the evidence and conclusions of such studies. "They should," he says, "be viewed as indicative of trends rather than as precise and accurate measures of current behavior."

Glossary

abortion: The termination, usually intentional, of a pregancy through surgery, drugs, or other means.

abstinence: The act of refraining from sexual intercourse.

AIDS: A sexually transmitted disease that weakens the immune system until it is unable to fight off infections and illnesses.

chlamydia: A sexually transmitted disease characterized by symptoms including, in women, vaginal discharge, vaginal bleeding between periods, and abdominal pain, and, in men, painful urination and a discharge from the penis. If untreated, complications can include damage to the reproductive organs and/or sterility.

contraception or birth control: The prevention of conception, the joining of the male sperm and female egg; usually accomplished by the use of contraceptives such as condoms or the oral birth control pill.

curriculum (plural is curricula): A particular course or program of study in an educational institution.

ejaculation: The discharge of semen, containing sperm, from the penis.

gay or homosexual: Often used in the general sense to include males strictly attracted to males; lesbians, or females strictly attracted to females; and bisexuals, or persons attracted to both males and females.

genital herpes: A sexually transmitted disease characterized by uncomfortable and infectious sores or blisters on the sex organs. The initial sores usually go away after five to ten days, and then re-erupt at regular or irregular intervals, depending on the individual.

genitals: The sex organs, specifically the male penis and testes, and the female vagina and clitoris.

genital warts or condyloma: An infection of the sex organs caused by the human papillomavirus (HPV) and spread by sexual contact. Genital warts are usually removed by surgery, freezing, or burning by electricity or lasers.

gonorrhea: A sexually transmitted disease characterized by symptoms including, in men, a burning sensation when urinating and/or a yellowish-white discharge from the penis, and, in women, a similar vaginal discharge. If untreated, complications can include sterility or arthritis in men and pelvic inflammatory disease in women; also called by slang terms, such as the "clap," "drip," "dose," and "strain."

heterosexuality: A sexual orientation in which a person is attracted to people of the opposite gender.

homosexuality: A sexual orientation in which a person is attracted to people of the same gender.

human immunodeficiency virus (HIV): The virus that causes AIDS. HIV is most often passed through sexual intercourse, both vaginal and anal, and through injections by infected needles.

miscarriage: Involuntary, premature loss of the fetus from the uterus during pregnancy.

pelvic inflammatory disease (PID): An infection of the female ovaries and/or fallopian tubes, often caused by untreated STDs such as gonorrhea; complications can include sterility and tubal pregnancies.

sexually transmitted diseases (STDs): Formerly referred to as venereal diseases (VD).

Organizations to Contact

The following organizations are concerned with issues discussed in this book. Most have publications or information available for interested readers. Because this list was compiled on the date of writing of the present volume, names, addresses, and phone numbers may have changed. Allow as much time as possible: Many organizations take several weeks or longer to respond to inquiries.

Advocates for Youth
1025 Vermont Ave. NW, Suite 210
Washington, DC 20005
(202) 347-5700

Advocates for Youth is an educational organization dedicated to improving the quality of life for adolescents by preventing teenage childbearing. Advocates for Youth's national and international programs seek to improve adolescent decision making through life-planning and other educational programs, to improve access to reproductive health care, to promote the development of school-based clinics, and to prevent the spread of HIV and other sexually transmitted diseases among adolescents. It publishes the quarterly *Clinic News* and *Options*, as well as fact sheets, reports, and resource guides.

The Alan Guttmacher Institute (AGI)
120 Wall St.
New York, NY 10005
(212) 248-1111

AGI works to develop effective family planning and sex education programs through policy analysis, public education, and research. The institute publishes the bimonthly *Family Planning Perspectives* and the quarterly *International Family Planning Perspectives*.

Children's Defense Fund (CDF)
25 East St. NW
Washington, DC 20001
(202) 628-8787

The CDF promotes the interests of children, especially poor, minority, and handicapped children. It supports government funding of education and health care policies for children. In addition to its monthly newsletter *CDF Reports*, the fund publishes many books, articles, and pamphlets, including *The Adolescent and Young Adult Fact Book* and *Adolescent Pregnancy: An Anatomy of a Social Problem in Search of Solutions*.

Concerned Women for America (CWA)
370 L'Enfant Promenade SW, Suite 800
Washington, DC 20024
(202) 488-7000

CWA lobbies Congress to pass laws that will strengthen the traditional nuclear family. It is opposed to government-funded day care and abortion. It publishes several brochures, including *Teen Pregnancy* and *School-Based Health Clinics*.

Focus on the Family
Colorado Springs, CO 80995
(719) 531-3400

Focus on the Family is a Christian conservative organization dedicated to preserving and strengthening the traditional family. It believes the breakdown of the traditional family is linked to increases in poverty, teen pregnancy, and drug abuse. It produces several radio programs and magazines as well as family-oriented books, films, videos, and audiocassettes. Among its publications are the monthly magazine *Focus on the Family* and the booklet *Teaching Your Kids to Say 'No' to Sex*.

The Hetrick-Martin Institute (HMI)
2 Astor Pl.
New York, NY 10003
(212) 674-2400

The Hetrick-Martin Institute offers a broad range of social services to gay and lesbian teenagers and their families. It also sponsors advocacy and education programs for gay and lesbian adolescents. HMI and the Child Welfare League of America cowrote the booklet *Serving Lesbian and Gay Youth*. Its publications also include the newsletter *HMI Report Card*, as well as articles, comic books, and pamphlets on homosexuality.

National Family Planning and Reproductive Health Association (NFPRHA)
122 C St. NW, Suite 380
Washington, DC 20001
(202) 628-3535

This association works to improve family planning and reproductive health services by acting as a national communications network. It publishes *NFPRHA News and Report* monthly, as well as various papers, including "The Effects of Sexual Education."

National Gay Youth Network
PO Box 846
San Francisco, CA 94101-0846

The network distributes educational materials for and about young lesbians, gays, and bisexuals. Its publications include *Helping Gay Youth: Problems and Possibilities* and *We Are Here*, a listing of community resources and services for gay and lesbian teens. Interested youth can obtain information by sending a stamped, self-addressed envelope to the above address.

Parents, Families, and Friends of Lesbians and Gays (PFLAG)
1101 14th St. NW, Suite 1030
Washington, DC 20005

(202) 638-4200
e-mail: pflagntl@aol.com

PFLAG is a national organization that provides support, education, and advocacy services for gays, lesbians, bisexuals, and their families and friends. It works to end prejudice and discrimination against gays, lesbians, and bisexuals. It publishes and distributes pamphlets and articles, including *Why Is My Child Gay?*, *About Our Children,* and *Coming Out to Your Parents.*

Planned Parenthood
810 Seventh Ave.
New York, NY 10019
(212) 541-7800

Planned Parenthood supports people who make their own decisions about having children without governmental interference. It provides contraceptive counseling and services through clinics located throughout the United States. Among its extensive publications are the brochures *Guide to Birth Control: Seven Accepted Methods of Contraception, It's Okay to Say No Way, Teensex?, A Man's Guide to Sexuality,* and *About Childbirth.*

Project Reality
PO Box 97
Golf, IL 60029
(708) 729-3298

Project Reality has developed a sex education curriculum for junior and senior high school students called Sex Respect. The program is designed to provide teenagers with information and to encourage sexual abstinence. According to the authors of the curriculum, "Sex Respect teaches teens that saying 'no' to premarital sex is their right, is in the best interest of society, and is in the spirit of true sexual freedom."

Reconciling Congregation Program (RCP)
3801 N. Keeler Ave.
Chicago, IL 60641
(312) 736-5526

RCP is a network of United Methodist churches that welcomes and supports lesbians and gay men and seeks to end homophobia and prejudice in the church and society. The national headquarters provides resources to help local ministries achieve these goals. Among its publications are the quarterly magazine *Open Hands*, the book *And God Loves Each One*, and pamphlets, studies, and videos.

Search Institute
Thresher Square West
700 S. Third St., Suite 210
Minneapolis, MN 55415-1138
(612) 376-8955

Search Institute is a nonprofit research organization dedicated to advancing the well-being of children and adolescents through scientific research, evaluation, consultation, and the development of practical resources. The institute has developed a values-based curriculum for the seventh and eighth grades titled *Human Sexuality: Values & Choices*. It publishes the quarterly newsletter *Source*, research reports, books, videos, curricula, study guides, and workbooks.

Sex Information and Education Council of the United States (SIECUS)
130 W. 42nd St., Suite 350
New York, NY 10036
(212) 819-9770

SIECUS supports the individual's right to acquire knowledge of sexuality and encourages the development of responsible standards of sexual behavior. This organization provides education, training, and leadership programs; it is one of the largest national clearinghouses for information on human sexuality. In addition to publishing sex education curricula, SIECUS also publishes a newsletter, *SIECUS Report*, and the books, *Adolescent Pregnancy and Parenthood* and *Oh No! What Do I Do Now?*

Suggestions for Further Reading

T. Allen, "Gay Students Speak Out," *Education Digest*, November 1995.

Michael D. Benson, *Coping with Birth Control*. New York: Rosen Publishing Group, 1992.

Sonia Bowe-Gutman, *Teen Pregnancy*. Minneapolis: Lerner Publications, 1987.

Mary S. Calderone and James W. Ramey, *Talking with Your Child About Sex: Questions and Answers for Children from Birth to Puberty*. New York: Ballantine Books, 1982.

Alex Comfort and Jane Comfort, *The Facts of Love: Living, Loving, and Growing Up*. New York: Ballantine Books, 1979.

Charles P. Cozic, ed., *Sexual Values: Opposing Viewpoints*. San Diego: Greenhaven Press, 1995.

Robie H. Harris, *It's Perfectly Normal: A Book About Changing Bodies, Growing Up, Sex, and Sexual Health*. Cambridge, MA: Candlewick Press, 1994.

"I'm HIV Positive," *Teen*, September 1995.

Mary Kittredge, *Teens with AIDS Speak Out*. Englewood Cliffs, NJ: Julian Messner, 1991.

R. Lanning, "He Only Wanted Me for Sex," *Teen*, August 1995.

Eric Marcus, *Is It a Choice? Answers to 300 of the Most Frequently Asked Questions About Gays and Lesbians*. San Francisco: Harper, 1993.

B. Mirsky, "Living with AIDS," *Sassy*, October 1995.

Joelle Sander, *Before Their Time: Four Generations of Teenage Mothers*. San Diego: Harcourt Brace Jovanovich, 1991.

Herma Silverstein, *Teenage and Pregnant: What You Can Do*. Englewood Cliffs, NJ: Julian Messner, 1988.

Works Consulted

Joseph Adelson, "Sex Among the Americans," *Commentary*, July 1995.

T. Allen, "Will Kids Buy Abstinence?" *Education Digest*, January 1995.

J. D. Anderson, "Including Gay/Lesbian Students and Staff," *Education Digest*, December 1994.

Bruce Bawer, *A Place at the Table: The Gay Individual in American Society*. New York: Poseidon Press, 1993.

S. Begley, "Nature Plus Nurture," *Newsweek*, November 13, 1995.

Neal Bernards, ed., *Teenage Sexuality: Opposing Viewpoints*. San Diego: Greenhaven Press, 1988.

L. A. Berne and B. K. Huberman, "Sexuality Education Works: Here's the Proof," *Education Digest*, February 1996.

Douglas J. Besharov, "Teen Sex," *The American Enterprise*, January/February 1993.

Francis Canavan, "The Sexual Revolution Explained," *The New Oxford Review*, November 1993.

P. Castro, "Facts of Life," *People Weekly*, November 13, 1995.

Ralph J. DiClemente, "Epidemiology of AIDS, HIV, Prevalence, and HIV Incidence Among Adolescents," *Journal of School Health*, September 1992.

B. Ehrenreich, "Put Your Pants On, Demonboy," *Time*, October 23, 1995.

"Fears and Facts," *Teen*, October 1995.

"For Fewer Abortions, We Need More Talk About Sex,"
Glamour, July 1995.

S. Gordon, "What Kids Need to Know," *Psychology Today*,
October 1986.

K. Hacker et al., "A Nationwide Survey of School Health
Services Delivery in Urban Schools," *Journal of School
Health*, September 1994.

Patricia Hersch, "Sex and the Boomers' Babies," *Family
Therapy Networker*, March/April 1993.

"Keeping Students on Track: Comprehensive Health Care
and Education for American Teenagers," *Ounce of
Prevention Fund*, 1994 Report.

D. Kirby, "School-Based Programs to Reduce Sexual Risk-
taking Behaviors," *Journal of School Health*, September
1992.

H. H. Kitasei, "STDs: What You Don't Know Can Hurt
You," *Ms.*, March/April 1995.

Simon LeVay and Dean H. Hamer, "Evidence for a
Biological Influence in Male Homosexuality," *Scientific
American*, May 1994.

Judith Levine, "Thinking About Sex," *Tikkun*, March 1988.

Gisela Meier, *Teenage Pregnancy*. New York: Marshall
Cavendish, 1994.

Robert T. Michael et al., *Sex in America: A Definitive
Survey*. Boston: Little, Brown and Company, 1994.

M. R. Neifert, "Why Teen Sex Is Riskier than Ever,"
McCall's, August 1995.

Susan Newcomer and Wendy Baldwin, "Demographics of
Adolescent Sexual Behavior, Contraception, Pregnancy, and
STDs," *Journal of School Health*, September 1992.

"No Dent at All in Teens' Birthrate," *Los Angeles Times*,
January 2, 1996.

J. Overbeck, "Sex, Kids, and the Slut Look," *Newsweek*, July 26, 1993.

W. Plummer and C. Rist, "Reality Bites," *People Weekly*, November 27, 1995.

Michael D. Resnick, "Adolescent Pregnancy Options," *Journal of School Health*, September 1992.

B. A. Rienzo, "Factors in the Successful Establishment of School-Based Clinics," *Clearing House*, July/August 1994.

B. A. Rienzo et al., "The Politics of School-Based Programs Which Address Sexual Orientation," *Journal of School Health*, January 1996.

Clark Robenstine, "AIDS Education for Black High-Schoolers," *Education Digest*, September 1995.

D. G. Savage, "Justices Reject School Condom Policy Challenge," *Los Angeles Times*, January 9, 1996.

M. Shaw, "Gay Pride in High School," *The Progressive*, July 1995.

Brenda Stalcup, ed., *Human Sexuality: Opposing Viewpoints*. San Diego: Greenhaven Press, 1995.

Karin L. Swisher, ed., *Teenage Sexuality: Opposing Viewpoints*. San Diego: Greenhaven Press, 1994.

"This Is What You Thought: How Much Sex Education Do Kids Need?" *Glamour*, July 1995.

L. Treadway and J. Yoakam, "Creating a Safer Environment for Lesbian and Gay Students," *Journal of School Health*, September 1992.

T. Watson and J. P. Shapiro, "Is There a Gay Gene?" *U.S. News & World Report*, November 13, 1995.

W. L. Yarber and A. V. Parrillo, "Adolescents and Sexually Transmitted Diseases," *Journal of School Health*, September 1992.

Laurie S. Zabin, *Adolescent Sexual Behavior and Childbearing*. Newbury Park, CA: Sage Publications, 1993.

Index

About the Author

Don Nardo is an award-winning author whose more than seventy books cover a wide range of topics. His historical overviews include *The Mexican-American War*, *The U.S. Presidency*, *Franklin D. Roosevelt*, *Braving the New World*, *The Battle of Marathon*, *Julius Caesar*, *The Age of Augustus*, and many others. In addition to this volume on teen sexuality, his other works on health and social issues include *The Physically Challenged*, *Eating Disorders*, *Drugs and Sports*, *Anxiety and Phobias*, *Vaccines*, *Vitamins and Minerals*, and *The Death Penalty*. Mr. Nardo also dabbles periodically in orchestral composition, oil painting, screenwriting, and film directing. He lives with his wife, Christine, on Cape Cod, Massachusetts.

Picture Credits

Cover photo: © Dan Habib/Impact Visuals
© Donna Binder/Impact Visuals, 72
© Amy Elliott, 48
© Harvey Finkle/Impact Visuals, 26
© 1995 Rick Gerharter/Impact Visuals, 65, 70
© Nate Guidry/Impact Visuals, 67
© Dan Habib/Impact Visuals, 9, 10, 13, 14, 19, 22, 35, 39,
   41, 51
© Phil Huber/Black Star, 52, 63
© Evan Johnson/Impact Visuals, 30, 53
© Katherine McGlynn/Impact Visuals, 24
© Paul L. Merideth, 57
© 1993 Linda Rosier/Impact Visuals, 8
© Blair Seitz/Photo Researchers, 75

SEPT 15th 2013

HAPPY BIRTHDAY
YOU! BEAUTIFUL
CHILD!
LONDON! WHERE
YOU VISITED
MILES AND YASMIN!
MUCH MUCH LOVE
X   X
♡ Zazard ♡
   o Lola o

London

Catriona Clarke

Designed by Tom Lalonde
Illustrated by Terry McKenna

London consultant: Hedley Swain, Museum of London
Reading consultant: Alison Kelly, Roehampton University

Contents